Middle East Today

Series Editors

The Iranian Revolution of 1979, the Iran-Iraq War, the Gulf War, and the US invasion and occupation of Iraq have dramatically altered the geopolitical landscape of the contemporary Middle East. The Arab Spring uprisings have complicated this picture. This series puts forward a critical body of first-rate scholarship that reflects the current political and social realities of the region, focusing on original research about contentious politics and social movements; political institutions; the role played by non-governmental organizations such as Hamas, Hezbollah, and the Muslim Brotherhood; and the Israeli-Palestine conflict. Other themes of interest include Iran and Turkey as emerging pre-eminent powers in the region, the former an 'Islamic Republic' and the latter an emerging democracy currently governed by a party with Islamic roots; the Gulf monarchies, their petrol economies and regional ambitions; potential problems of nuclear proliferation in the region; and the challenges confronting the United States, Europe, and the United Nations in the greater Middle East. The focus of the series is on general topics such as social turmoil, war and revolution, international relations, occupation, radicalism, democracy, human rights, and Islam as a political force in the context of the modern Middle East.

Samantha Louden-Cooke

Gender Equality, Matrimony, and Secularism in Egypt and Iran: A Comparative Exploration of Early Twentieth-Century Family Law

palgrave
macmillan

Samantha Louden-Cooke
University of Gloucestershire
Cheltenham, UK

ISSN 2945-7017 ISSN 2945-7025 (electronic)
Middle East Today
ISBN 978-3-032-00845-9 ISBN 978-3-032-00846-6 (eBook)
https://doi.org/10.1007/978-3-032-00846-6

Cover credit: Mikadun Shutterstock.com

This Palgrave Macmillan imprint is published by the registered company Springer Nature Switzerland AG
The registered company address is: Gewerbestrasse 11, 6330 Cham, Switzerland

For Tom & Pipps, who make everything worthwhile.

Acknowledgements They say it takes a village to raise a family; the same is true for projects like this. This book, a decade in the making and rooted in my doctoral research, would not have come to life without the support and patience of many extraordinary people. I am deeply grateful to Palgrave Macmillan for giving it a home.

To my friends, family, and colleagues, thank you. Your advice, patience, and encouragement, especially during the more difficult moments, have been invaluable. Jennifer, Nat, Nicola, Kenny, Rosina, Maxine, Justin, Cat, Alexia, Ceri, Omar, and Rachel, you have all supported me in so many different ways, whether reading draft, being a sounding board, or just being there and it means so much.

A heartfelt thanks goes to Alireza, my Persian tutor, who has not only supported my language learning but also generously assisted with the transliteration and translation of Persian terms. To Duha, who kindly volunteered her time to help with Arabic translations and transliterations; you truly exemplify the kindness of strangers, and I am sincerely thankful.

And to Tom, I may never fully understand your endless patience with me, particularly during peak stress, but I will not question it. I love you more than you know.

To everyone mentioned here, and to those whose support has been no less vital, even if unnamed, thank you.

You are all awesome-sauce and your support means the world to me.

Competing Interests The author has no competing interests to declare that are relevant to the content of this manuscript.

Note on Transliteration and Translation

In this book, both standard Arabic and standard Persian terms are used. Transliterations are loosely based on the IJMES transliteration guide for both languages. Diacritical marks have been included for transliterations and Arabic translations. Translations are my inclusion, where they are by citations, they are not attributed to that author. Accuracy of translations and transliterations has been sought with native speakers, also fluent in English, proofing the author's work. While all measures have been taken to ensure accuracy, any mistakes are my own. Inconsistencies in transliteration throughout may reflect the inclusion of quotes.

CONTENTS

Abbreviations

EFU	Egyptian Feminist Union
FIS	Front Islamique du Salut
	Foundation for Iranian Studies
IRI	Islamic Republic of Iran
MENA	Middle East/North Africa
NLS	National Ladies Society
NWRO	Network of Women's Rights Organisation
TNA	The National Archives

Introduction: Power, Agency, and Identity

Marriage, as a social institution, manifests differently across states, cultures, religions, and individual contexts. In some settings, it continues to draw heavily from traditional norms; in others, it has undergone notable transformations. Yet access to and engagement with these changes remain uneven, often constrained by a complex web of state and familial controls. Matrimonial equality, and the structures that inhibit or enable it, are best understood through five intersecting paradigms: (a) state law; (b) cultural practice; (c) religion; (d) secularism; and (e) the family. These domains shape not only how marriages begin but also how they are maintained and eventually ended—whether through divorce or death—with *Sharīʿah* (الشريعة; Shari'a) law maintaining significant influence across many Muslim-majority societies.

What is often lost in mainstream discourse are the nuances within Muslim marital systems. Muslim marriages are frequently treated as monolithic, reinforcing stereotypes that link Islam with dangerous and degrading stereotypes. These homogenising narratives obscure the varied and evolving realities within Muslim-majority states. Understanding developments in matrimonial equality requires attention to how these five paradigms interact within specific legal and cultural settings. This book adopts such a lens in comparing gendered experiences of marriage

S. Louden-Cooke, *Gender Equality, Matrimony and Secularism in Egypt and Iran: A Comparative Exploration of Early Twentieth-Century Family Law*, Middle East Today,
https://doi.org/10.1007/978-3-032-00846-6_1

in Egypt and Iran, particularly during the early twentieth century, when both states experienced significant legal and ideological shifts.

Egypt and Iran offer a compelling comparative study in how (semi-) colonial states navigated modernisation, nationalism, and social reform under the shadow of foreign domination. While Egypt endured formal British occupation and Iran retained nominal sovereignty, both nations operated within the constraints of imperial interests that shaped their internal politics and economic dependencies. In Egypt, British control over the Suez Canal and cotton economy limited the scope of nationalist reforms despite gaining quasi-independence in 1922, while simultaneously contributing to a marriage crisis (Kholoussy, 2003, 2010). In Iran, the Anglo-Persian Oil Company's control of oil production functioned as a lever of informal empire, fuelling nationalist resentment even as *Reza Šah Pahlavi* (رضا شاه پهلوی; Reza Shah Pahlavi) consolidated power, however, British imperialism pre-dated the discovery of oil.

Their political trajectories diverged too, with Egypt's 1919 revolution producing a quasi-parliamentary system and a pluralistic political culture, whereas Iran's 1906 Constitutional Revolution gave way to authoritarian centralisation under *Reza Šah* by the mid-1920s. Yet both states, in different ways, exposed the paradox of modernity imposed from above: infrastructural and educational expansion occurred alongside persistent political exclusion.

This paradox was sharply visible in the domain of gender equality and family law. In Egypt, while feminist voices such as Huda Sha'arawi's challenged patriarchal norms and formed institutions like the Egyptian Feminist Union, *sharīʿah* (الشريعة; sharia)-based family law remained largely intact and continued to constrain women's legal agency in areas such as divorce and child custody. Iran, by contrast, displaced religious courts in favour of a secular judiciary and enforced unveiling in 1936, projecting an image of gender progressivism. Yet these reforms were largely symbolic: family law continued to reinforce male authority, and women were denied substantive legal rights. While *sharīʿah* structured family law, adherence to different Schools—with Egypt following the *Hanafī* branch of Sunni Islam, and Iran following *Šiʿeh-yi Ithnā ʿAshari* (Twelver Shi'ism; شیعه‌ی اثنا عشری)—resulted in different rights for individuals in all stages of marriage and its ending.

These contrasts reveal not simply differences in state relations with colonial powers, but also how secularism was introduced and modernity constructed within different cultural and political environments.

Despite their differences, however, both states deployed legal and social tools to reinforce gendered hierarchies. Power structures—operating through legal, religious, and domestic environments—shaped the contours of women's agency in distinct but parallel ways. These histories are not static, rather they navigate complexities of state and individual identities within the context of the colonial era. Moreover, the marital union between both states following the marriage of Princess Fawzia of Egypt, and Muhammed Reza Khan of Iran in 1939 (Sabit, 1989) illuminates the unique intertwining of two states, distinct in both history, approaches to family law, and religious identities.

Recent state responses to popular dissent reflect deeper, enduring patterns, revealing the persistent role of the state in regulating gender and resisting challenges to its authority. By comparing these trajectories within broader regional contexts, this book sheds light on how law, religion, and power intersect to structure marriage, and how individuals continue to navigate, and resist, those structures in pursuit of equality.

Iranian Agency

On 16 September 2022, widespread protests erupted across Iran following the death of 22-year-old Mahsa Amini, who died while in the custody of the *gašt-e eršâd* (گشت ارشاد; morality police). Detained for allegedly violating Iran's strict dress code by wearing her hijab 'improperly', Amini's death became a flashpoint, galvanising citizens—particularly women—into action. Public demonstrations quickly transformed into a nationwide expression of dissent, with women discarding their headscarves, cutting their hair in public, and chanting slogans that called for justice, bodily autonomy, and an end to authoritarian control.

The *gašt-e eršâd*, established in 2005 as the successor to earlier Islamic enforcement bodies, exemplify the state's institutionalised control over women's bodies and behaviour. Through their surveillance and punishment of perceived moral transgressions, they have become a key instrument in the broader apparatus of gender-based repression. The protests, sparked by Amini's death, evolved into a broader challenge to state authority. Demonstrators called not only for the abolition of the *gašt-e eršâd* and the relaxation of mandatory veiling laws but also for structural change, including the removal of the Supreme Leader and accountability for systemic human rights abuses. The movement highlighted the power of grassroots mobilisation in confronting entrenched systems of oppression.

Despite gaining significant international attention, the Iranian government responded with heightened repression. By 4 April 2023, it was estimated that at least 19,200 individuals had been detained and 537 protesters killed (Loft, 2023). Eyewitness accounts and human rights reports documented the deliberate targeting of protesters' eyes and faces by security forces, resulting in hundreds being permanently blinded—physical scars that now serve as enduring symbols of dissent (UN, 2024).

The fate of those incarcerated at Evin Prison, notorious for holding political prisoners, became of grave concern on 16 October 2022 when a fire broke out in the facility, with links to the demonstrations being unclear (Ghobadi et al., 2022). What remains clear, however, is the continued use of state power to supress individual agency, and the disproportional responses to those challenging them. A core issue shaping political resistance in Iran is gender equality, in both the public and private spheres, with all aspects of political, private, and cultural life being intertwined with the rigid regime policies. This reinforces the prominence of patriarchal power structures across all aspects of Iranian society, evidencing the complexities of power formations within which public and private lives operate.

Power in this context is not abstract; it takes shape in lived experiences and hierarchical arrangements that structure both public life and personal relationships. Yoder and Kahn's (1992, 382–86) three-part framework brings this into focus: *power-over*, *interpersonal power-over*, and *power-to. Power-over*, as described by Goodrich (1991, cited in Yoder & Kahn, 1992), encapsulates domination—whether direct or indirect—exerted by one group over another, across societal, organisational, interpersonal, and individual domains. In Iran, this power-over emerges vividly in the gendered limitations imposed on women, from political exclusions to legal inequalities. *Interpersonal power-over* captures the everyday dynamics in relationships—such as marriage—where one individual's influence shapes the other's experience, even down to personality traits (Yoder & Kahn, 1992, 382–384). Finally, *power-to* describes the internal force of personal agency—the sense of control over one's own emotions, actions, and thoughts (Yoder & Kahn, 1992, 384). Positioned in opposition to *power-over*, it embodies the very thing the regime attempts to stifle.

As the complexities of the unrest in Iran continue, these different types of power and their mechanics become increasingly visible. Moreover, perceptions of women as inferior to men are exemplified, not only through expectations about their presentation in public, as we are seeing with the current protests, but also their presence in public. The constraints imposed on women in contemporary Iran can be traced directly to the political reconfigurations following the Islamic Revolution of 1979. While the ideological framing differed from that of the Pahlavi era, the marginalisation of women persisted, albeit through renewed mechanisms of state control. These continuities became particularly visible on the international stage following Ghoncheh Ghavami's arrest in June 2014. Her peaceful protest—challenging the banning of female spectators at volleyball matches—served as a poignant illustration of the enduring influence of patriarchal structures within Iranian society. It exemplified what Yoder and Kahn (1992) term *power-over*, wherein hierarchical systems, legitimised through governmental discourse, actively restrict individual agency based on gendered logics.

The global attention garnered by Ghoncheh's case stemmed not only from the act of protest itself but from the disproportionate response it elicited. A British-Iranian law graduate from the School of Oriental and African Studies, University of London—and herself a volleyball player—Ghoncheh was initially detained while protesting the state-imposed ban on women attending volleyball matches. This ban, introduced in 2012, echoed similar prohibitions enacted post-1979, under the justification that women required protection from the 'lewd behaviour' of male spectators at stadium games (Amnesty International, 2014). Such rhetoric underscores how gendered stereotypes of female vulnerability are instrumentalised to legitimise exclusionary policies. Despite not relating to her peaceful protest, she was later re-arrested on what her mother says the authorities recognised as unrelated charges (The Guardian, 2014), spending approximately five months in Tehran's Evin Prison—part of which was in solitary confinement. Although released on bail in November 2014 and cleared of all charges in 2015, Ghoncheh remained barred from leaving Iran for a further two years (Kamali Dehgan, 2015).

This case not only highlights the severity of state repression but also illustrates how institutional discourse perpetuates binary constructions of masculinity and femininity—strength and weakness—that reinforce gender-based hierarchies. These discursive formations are embedded at both societal and organisational levels, reflecting systemic *power-over* dynamics that regulate women's presence in public spaces.

Moreover, these gendered power structures traverse class boundaries and are historically entrenched. The practice of early marriage for girls, for instance, has long served as a symbol of familial honour and economic consolidation, with younger brides often perceived as more malleable within patriarchal structures. This dynamic is evident in the lives of historical figures such as Princess Taj al-Sultaneh (1883–1936) and Sattareh Farman Farmaian (1921–2012), whose early experiences were shaped by polygamous family settings. Taj was betrothed at the age of nine and married by thirteen, while Sattareh, the thirteenth of thirty-six children, was born to a mother who had been married at twelve. These narratives illustrate how deeply entrenched familial and political hierarchies shaped—and continue to shape—women's roles within both private and public spheres.

The continued relegation of women to the domestic domain and their systematic exclusion from public life, whether through legal prohibition or the silencing of dissent, reflects a persistent strategy of containment. It is through these practices that the state reaffirms patriarchal authority, attempting not only to discipline the body but to delineate the very boundaries of acceptable female presence in the Iranian public sphere.

Egyptian Agency

Imprisonment as a tool to suppress dissent remains a prevalent feature of contemporary Egypt, particularly for women whose social mobility and personal agency are circumscribed by overlapping structures of patriarchal authority. These include not only formal legal systems, but also familial hierarchies and socio-religious norms that collectively regulate women's bodies and decisions. The historical persistence of such '(interpersonal) power-over' structures has been met with resistance across time, often led by prominent women who navigated—and disrupted—these constraints in striking ways.

Figures such as Huda Shaʿarawi (1879–1947) and Doria Shafik (1908–1975) challenged prevailing gender norms by initiating separations from their husbands and, notably, refusing *mahr* (مَهْرٌ; dower), acts that redefined the symbolic and legal boundaries of marriage. Nawal El Saadawi (1931–2021) went further in asserting autonomy through multiple divorces, unwavering pursuit of education, and a prolific body of (autobiographical) writing. Together, these women illustrate the evolution of feminist consciousness in Egypt throughout the twentieth and twenty-first centuries, situating the personal as inherently political in an environment increasingly defined by surveillance and suppression.

The tension between state and citizen intensified in the wake of the 2011 uprisings—a period of both revolutionary optimism and institutional backlash. The brief ascendancy of the Muslim Brotherhood, culminating in Mohamed Morsi's presidency, ushered in heightened anxieties around gender and control. Public reports pointed to an increase in sexual violence targeting (non) Egyptian women as mechanisms for reinforcing a rigid gendered division between public and private space. These incidents were not isolated, but part of a long-standing dichotomisation of gender roles in Egyptian political life, frequently legitimised through religious discourse.

Though Morsi was Egypt's first democratically elected president, his administration lasted a year before being ousted in a military coup on 3 July 2013. During this short tenure, female protestors were frequently subjected to violence, including sexual assault, in what many saw as a deliberate effort to deter women from participating in public life. This more conservative turn in governance extended its reach to non-Egyptian women as well—Lara Logan, a CBS journalist, was among those assaulted while covering the 2011 protests, highlighting the transnational implications of state-sanctioned gendered violence (Maerz, 2011).

Sexual violence in this context functions as more than a tool of physical harm—it is a mechanism for stripping agency, asserting control, and delineating the boundaries of permissible dissent. The targeting of women's rights defenders illustrates the depth of state anxiety about autonomous individuals and organisations. The case of Azza Soliman, whose assets were frozen prior to her arrest alongside 15 others, reveals the systematic branding of human rights advocates as threats to national security. Case 173, which accused NGOs of foreign collusion, stands as a stark reminder of how legal and bureaucratic tools are mobilised to stifle resistance and consolidate authority (Amnesty International, 2017).

Rather than isolated acts, these developments represent a broader pattern. The forms of suppression may shift—through surveillance, asset seizure, sexual violence, or incarceration—but the underlying impulse to control, especially where women challenge dominant narratives, remains a central feature of the Egyptian state's engagement with dissent. Within this ongoing contestation, the experiences of activists, journalists, and everyday citizens create a fragmented but enduring mosaic of struggle and resilience.

Within Egypt's private sphere, the interplay of religious, legal, cultural, and economic power structures has shifted over time, shaping how successive generations interpret and engage with tradition, family law, and religious norms. These structures do not remain static; they respond to broader socio-political currents, particularly in relation to marriage. One such response has been the growing prevalence of *ʿirfīyy* (عرْفِيّ; not registered marriage) marriages.[1] While these marriages can be seen as strategies to navigate prohibitions on pre-marital relationships, they also reflect 'The costs of a regular marriage and the obligations that go with it…' (Knell, 2010).

The popularity of *ʿirfīyy* marriages is often attributed to economic hardship. For many, particularly among Egypt's youth, financial burdens—including housing, *mahr*, and ceremonial expenses—render formal marriage increasingly inaccessible. In poorer areas like Assiut, a 2006 survey indicated that the cost of a traditional marriage could equal up to fifteen times a household's annual income (Bohn, 2013). Such financial realities intersect with religious and social norms to influence who is deemed 'marriageable', reinforcing gendered expectations around financial provision, respectability, and familial suitability.

While legally recognised since 2000, *ʿirfīyy* marriages present complex legal and social consequences, especially for women. The case of actors Zeina and Ahmed Ezz drew widespread attention to these tensions. Despite DNA evidence confirming paternity, Ezz initially denied fathering Zeina's child, highlighting the precarious legal position of women in *ʿirfīyy* arrangements (Lambert & Ramadan, 2015). Without formal legal documentation, women face significant hurdles in establishing paternal responsibility or claiming rights related to inheritance and child support.

Parallels can be drawn between *ʿirfīyy* marriages in Egypt and *sigheh* (صيغه; temporary marriages) in Iran. Both forms offer religiously sanctioned alternatives to formal marriage while reinforcing patriarchal structures, particularly in the ease with which they can be dissolved and the limited obligations placed on men. *Sigheh* marriages often include a set duration—ranging from hours to years—further emphasising the transactional and gendered nature of these unions.

[1] *ʿIrfīyy* marriages are becoming more commonplace as a way to engage in sexual relations without the legal rights of a marriage, or the social connotations of pre-marital sex. This type of marriage requires two witnesses, but it not registered by legal or religious authorities.

The flexibility of these marriage forms reveals an ongoing renegotiation of family structures and gender roles within rapidly changing socio-economic contexts. However, such shifts are frequently met with resistance, particularly when they challenge entrenched norms regarding male authority, female sexuality, and the sanctity of the traditional family unit. The persistence and precarity of these intersecting power structures—legal, religious, familial, and economic—complicate efforts to reimagine equitable relationships. Yet, mapping their dynamics is crucial for understanding the possibilities and limits of transformation within contemporary Egyptian and Iranian societies.

Patriarchy and Power Structures

This book argues that while family law in Egypt and Iran remained formally grounded in interpretations of *Sharī'ah*, the introduction and evolution of secularism significantly shaped gender equality within these legal frameworks. Rather than assessing secularism through the binary of its full or partial adoption, the analysis focuses on how secular principles were introduced, negotiated, and localised within each state's political and social fabric. This approach requires a careful consideration of the broader context: colonial entanglements, state formation processes, resistance movements, and the linguistic accessibility of historical and legal sources.

Edward Said (1978) provides a foundational lens for understanding the colonial logics that positioned Egypt as a linchpin of British imperial strategy. Its geographic centrality made it a critical conduit between the metropole and India, aligning with the broader imperial strategy of securing 'stepping-stones' across the region. Iran, by contrast, presents a compelling contrast, with its interactions with British imperialism having unfolded along different lines. Both countries introduced formal constitutions in the early twentieth century, offering a comparative frame for examining the institutionalisation of secularism and its differential impact on gendered legal norms. The distinct modalities of secular engagement in Egypt and Iran underpin the models developed in this work (see also Cooke, 2020 & 2021; Louden-Cooke, 2024), illuminating both the intentions of state actors and the reactions of citizens—especially women—towards the unfolding secular projects.

Colonial impositions, often couched in discourses of modernity and superiority, are inextricably linked to these secular transformations. Engaging these histories through a postcolonial feminist lens not only situates women within the political economy of imperialism but also critiques the ways in which their agency has been obscured or flattened. This book adopts the perspective advanced by Mohanty (1988) in her critique of Zed Press' *Women in the Third World* series, where she underscores the dangers of homogenising women's experiences with patriarchal power structures and these frameworks, she reinforces the need for more reflective and reflexive engagements to occur between Western feminist works on non-Western women. Instead of reproducing generalisations, this book adopts a reflexive methodology—one that foregrounds some women's own negotiations with both religious and secular paradigms.

Yet, despite the influence of Said's work, critiques such as those by Abu-Lughod (2001) point to a notable absence: women's experiences under Orientalism remain under-theorised. The legacy of orientalist discourse continues to shape global perceptions of Muslim women, framing them as passive subjects of an oppressive Islamic order. These representations have often reinforced assumptions within Western feminist discourse that overlook the agency and multiplicity of non-Western women's lived realities. Moreover, Orientalist narratives have impacted not only external understandings of Muslim women but also the rights afforded to them, as filtered through the colonial and postcolonial state's legal apparatuses.

This exclusion parallels broader global patterns of gendered spatial control, wherein women are symbolically and legally confined to the private sphere, while men traverse both private and public domains. Such distinctions have long informed Western feminist debates and echo in non-Western contexts, suggesting that patriarchy—though expressed differently—transcends borders. In Islamic thought, the family is often cast as the moral and social cornerstone of society (Qutb, 2001, 25), with marriage as its foundation. Given this centrality, marriage and the family become key sites for examining how intersecting power structures—religious, legal, colonial, and economic—mediate women's roles and rights.

Rather than positing secularism as a straightforward solution to gender inequality, which of course it is not, this book argues that secular interventions in family law create alternative, not necessarily more expansive, configurations of women's rights. These outcomes depend heavily on the modes of secular engagement and the historical-political context of their implementation. Tracing women's evolving relationship to the state through family law thus enables a more nuanced understanding of both the constraints and the possibilities embedded in religious legal systems.

An historical approach to women's rights and legal reform is essential for excavating the specificities of state formation and gender politics in Egypt and Iran. It also enables a critique of dominant assumptions, particularly those that rely on essentialist portrayals of Islam as monolithically oppressive. Scholars such as Abu-Lughod (2001), Ahmed (1992), and Badran (1996, 2009) have challenged these portrayals, calling for contextualised and historically grounded analyses. Echoing Said's (1978, 84) observation that Egypt was cast as the symbolic key to both Asia and Africa, the discourse of Orientalism reveals how colonial powers imposed a singular identity on a region rich with cultural and religious diversity. The very term 'Middle East', as Tripp (2013, 17) notes, illustrates this flattening of difference—a geopolitical invention that bundled disparate societies into a unified other. This book seeks to deconstruct such narratives by foregrounding the diverse and contingent experiences of women within Islamic family law and secular reform in two culturally diverse states.

Postcolonial Feminist Considerations

To fully appreciate the impact of actors on gender equality and family law, it is useful to explore the intersecting identities and power structures which emerge throughout postcolonial feminist literature. By reflecting on individual positions and identities within society, greater understanding of the individual and the impact of power structures on them, or their impact on power structures, becomes more visible. One area of mutual agreement is that this oppression is not stagnant, rather the causes of oppression and the means by which it is believed to be alterable varies between feminist theories (Stanley & Wise 1993).

The interpretive imperative at the heart of feminist scholarship insists not only on recognising women's experiences but on unsettling the frameworks through which those experiences have historically been defined. In this regard, Stanley and Wise (1993, 118) argue that the act of reinterpreting the world—previously categorised through male-centric epistemologies—is central to feminist practice, a challenge that places lived experience in direct contestation with the detached objectivity prized by positivist traditions. Yet, while this theoretical repositioning of the personal as political has proved foundational, its application has not been universally inclusive. The voices foregrounded in early feminist theory often reflected the perspectives of white, Western, middle-class women—privileging particular modes of struggle while marginalising others. Women from racialised, socio-economically disadvantaged, or colonised contexts have long pointed to the ways in which this dominant feminism failed to speak to their realities, even as it claimed universality (Agathangelou & Turcotte, 2010, 50).

Critiques of what has been termed 'hegemonic feminism' do not merely stem from a theoretical divergence—they arise from experiences of misrecognition and erasure. When Western feminist narratives circulate globally, often stripped of historical specificity, they risk becoming misaligned with the priorities and expressions of gendered resistance in other locales. The tensions are not abstract. In various postcolonial contexts, the term 'feminism' itself can provoke suspicion—seen as a foreign import, an ideological extension of Western modernity, rather than an organic development within local struggles. Yet, this reading is not uncontested. Jayawardena (1986) systematically dismantles the idea that feminist consciousness in the Global South is an external imposition, instead tracing its emergence through indigenous reform movements, anti-colonial activism, and locally embedded critiques of gendered power. These histories complicate any linear or geographically fixed account of feminist development, revealing instead a textured landscape of convergences, refusals, and reinventions.

Feminist movements emerging in non-Western contexts are frequently positioned within singular or totalising frameworks which often obscure their specific political and cultural textures. Egypt offers a particularly illustrative case, where feminist organising was historically shaped not only by secular nationalism but also by social class and divergent ideological currents. El Guindi (2003, 591) draws attention to Badran's identification of early Egyptian feminism as secular—a terrain largely occupied by upper-and middle-class women whose activism was intertwined with nationalist aspirations. However, Ahmed's intervention complicates this characterisation by disaggregating the movement into two identifiable strands: one associated with Huda Shaarawi and bearing clear traces of Western feminist idioms; the other, exemplified by Malak Hifni Nasif, rooted in a more indigenous intellectual tradition that sought reform without recourse to Western paradigms (El Guindi, 2003, 591). In this way, Egyptian feminism did not simply reflect imported categories but developed through internal tensions and historically contingent negotiations.

Despite recognition of the Egyptian movement as secular, feminist scholarship on women in the MENA region remains persistently filtered through the twin lenses of religion and tradition (Lazreg, 1988, 84). Lazreg (1988) notes that academic narratives often cast women's experiences within a static religio-cultural paradigm, flattening the political complexities that define their lives. The family, positioned within religio-legal frameworks, becomes the assumed site of both subjugation and reform—an 'automated' locus through which gender is interpreted. This narrowing of focus does not simply misrepresent women's lives; it reifies the very binaries that feminist inquiry seeks to disrupt.

To bring these historically situated narratives into dialogue with the contemporary requires attending to the reshaping of feminist critique under globalisation. Hegde (1998, 272) identifies this shift as a product of feminist, poststructuralist, and postcolonial thought intersecting in newly emergent spaces of critique. The increasing entanglement of local struggles with transnational forces has prompted calls, such as those by Alexander and Mohanty (cited in McEwan, 2001, 106), for a 'comparative, relational feminist praxis that is transnational in its response to, and engagement with, global processes of colonisation'—one that resists the universalising pull of Western feminist assumptions and instead acknowledges the multiplicity of feminist genealogies and agendas.

In this context, methodological critiques take on particular salience. Mohanty (2003a, 62) highlights a recurring tendency in Western feminist research to establish the universality of patriarchy by measuring the frequency of gendered oppression. This form of reasoning neglects context, agency, and meaning, reducing complex cultural practices to simplistic symbols in a preconfigured narrative—implying, for example, that the prevalence of veiling among Muslim women confirms its status as an emblem of subjugation.

Such critiques are amplified by postcolonial theorists, who problematise the authority of Western epistemologies over non-Western subjects (Briggs, J & Sharp, 2004). The work of Said (1978) and others has illuminated how colonial knowledge systems became enmeshed with global structures of power, shaping not only how the 'Other' was known, but also how Western modernity understood itself (Briggs & Sharp, 2004,

663). Postcolonial feminists extend this analysis by examining how gendered subjects are rendered intelligible—or not—within these systems. The concern is not simply that non-Western women are misrepresented, but that they are often spoken *for*, situated within discourses that do not permit the articulation of their own frameworks of meaning (Briggs & Sharp, 2004, 664).

This critique dovetails with broader efforts to decentralise the West as the epistemic centre. Hegde (1998, 281) links the privileging of Western knowledge to Enlightenment-era commitments to universalism, which found easy expression in colonial modes of classification and control. Postcolonial feminism responds by displacing these hierarchies—dismantling binary oppositions between the centre and periphery, and instead situating knowledge as produced through entangled histories and uneven power relations. The aim is not merely to add new voices, but to disrupt the structures that previously silenced them.

A feminist analysis rooted in postcolonial theory necessarily turns attention to the intersectional dynamics of race, class, gender, and imperial history. As Tickner and Sjoberg (2013, 212) argue, it is at these intersections that the exclusions of mainstream feminism become most visible. Chakraborty (2007, 106) goes further, describing Western feminism as a kind of nation-state—its boundaries policed by the binaries of insider/outsider, inclusion/exclusion. Within this paradigm, the 'racially experiencing subject' becomes a perpetual outsider, marked by difference. This critique resonates with the concerns raised by Nawal El Saadawi, who condemned the myopic focus of Western feminists on sexuality and patriarchy while neglecting material conditions shaped by class and colonial histories (Amireh, 2000, 220).

Postcolonial feminists thus aim not only to challenge representations but to contest the authority to name, theorise, and define. The persistence of colonial logics in feminist thought—where black and brown women continue to be othered, essentialised, or omitted—demands more than mere inclusion. It calls for epistemic reorientation. As McEwan (2001, 100) notes, Western feminist depictions of non-Western women have changed little since the colonial era. Against this backdrop, Lewis and Mills (2003, 3) describe postcolonial feminism as a dual intervention: first, to racialise mainstream feminism, and second, to embed feminist concerns within critiques of colonialism and postcolonial governance. Yet even this duality risks becoming reductive if it collapses into a formulaic 'add women and stir' approach (Mohanty, 2003b, 518).

Nevertheless, by foregrounding mechanisms of exclusion—both within feminist theory and the geopolitical structures it engages—postcolonial feminism creates the conditions for more rigorous, reflective, and responsive modes of analysis. Sa'ar (2005, 683) underscores the necessity of incorporating these exclusionary dynamics into feminist frameworks, not simply to widen the field of analysis, but to deepen its ethical and political integrity.

Colonial, Secular, and Familial Powers

Postcolonial feminist theory situates gender within a matrix of political, historical, and epistemological entanglements where power is not simply a force but a process—both diffuse and strategic. Connell (1987, 107) frames power as a 'pattern of constraint on social practice', a dynamic that stretches beyond institutional control to the fundamental question of survival itself. Foucault (1982, 794) similarly conceptualises power as embedded within 'strategies of struggle', rather than possessed or monopolised—a confrontation played out across axes such as coloniser/colonised, and through the deeply sedimented asymmetries of gender. These relations are rarely static; they circulate, mutate, and are met with resistance, often subtle and oblique. In this regard, Scott's (1985) theory of 'weapons of the weak' gives form to the 'hidden transcripts' through which those rendered voiceless express agency, revealing acts of subversion lodged within everyday interactions (Briggs & Sharp, 2004, 666).

Power, within postcolonial feminist thought, cannot be disentangled from knowledge. Foucault's (cited in Lewis & Mills 2003, 1) assertion that knowledge is always implicated in systems of power challenges the notion of neutral or universal truths. The production of knowledge, far from a benign or objective endeavour, functions through inclusion and exclusion, naming and silencing. In the postcolonial context, this insight sharpens. As Hegde (1998, 284) notes, theoretical interventions grounded in poststructuralist critique unravel the normative categories of identity formation, pushing back against colonial myths 'inscribed in white ink'—a spectral authority that continues to script global hierarchies.

Yet such critiques are incomplete without attention to lived experience. Bell hooks (1984, 59) underscores the heterogeneity of racial and gendered identities, cautioning against essentialist readings that obscure differences even among women of shared ethnic backgrounds.

Experience, here, is not anecdotal but epistemic—it carries the weight of knowing otherwise, unsettling dominant frames from within. The omission of such differentiated accounts by mainstream feminist theory has drawn enduring criticism, particularly from voices located outside Western academic institutions. Yet as hooks (1984, 84) observes, feminist discourses have not always been consistent in their treatment of power. Some women, while resisting male domination, simultaneously articulate desires for parity within male-defined hierarchies, seeking equality without challenging the underlying logic of control.

Nowhere is this more evident than in the discourse of hegemonic masculinity. Connell's (1987, 183) analysis reveals the interaction of multiple masculinities, hierarchised and contested, which function to sustain patriarchal dominance not just over women but among men. As Cohn (2013, 4) underscores, hegemonic masculinity is a relational construct, legitimising particular expressions of male power while marginalising others. At the micro level, Kaufman (1994, 59) identifies control—over space, others, and emotion—as a key marker of masculinity. He further argues that this capacity is not innate but historically produced, gaining legitimacy through normative narratives that cast male dominance as 'natural' (Kaufman, 1994, 63).

The family, in this schema, becomes more than a private unit; it is a microcosm of wider social order. It encodes, performs, and reproduces patriarchal logics, not only through its hierarchical structuring but also through its role in normalising what Kaufman (1994, 63) calls '"normal" manhood'. Thus, the family emerges as a site where gendered power is both enacted and learnt—a formation that postcolonial feminist theory urges us to interrogate not as static, but as historically contingent and culturally variable.

Family

The family, long positioned as the nucleus of social organisation, extends beyond its institutional confines—particularly marriage—into feminist critiques of the relational interface between individuals and society. Stanley and Wise (1993, 93) suggest that it is within the familial context that prevailing norms and values are naturalised, rendering women integral to the maintenance of the social system. However, this apparent centrality is complicated by their observation that women are frequently 'added' into pre-existing frameworks, rather than these frameworks being reconstituted to account for gendered absences and silences (Stanley & Wise 1993, 118). The paradox of women's importance to social reproduction is sharpened when viewed historically through the lens of the public/private dichotomy—a distinction repeatedly problematised by feminists. As Mills (2003, 698) notes, scholars such as Milroy and Wismer have challenged the fusion of gender with spatial spheres, advocating for the decoupling of these entrenched binaries.

The categorisation of the family within the private realm is itself fraught. Anthias (2002, 280) points to the inconsistent placement of institutions such as religion, which are often relegated to the private sphere despite their enduring public presence.

As a site of both reproduction and regulation, the family functions as a power structure that not only reflects but also sustains broader social orders. Connell (1987, 121) refers to its ideological positioning as the 'foundation of society', a conceptualisation that obscures the power dynamics embedded in familial decision-making. Accordingly, the family emerges as a crucial site through which feminist theorists have examined women's oppression (Stanley & Wise, 1993, 75).

While the mechanisms of subjugation are widely acknowledged, feminist theorists diverge on the causes of and solutions to such oppression. What unites them, however, is the recognition of patriarchy as a pervasive and structuring force. Shail (2007, 88) highlights the complexities introduced by male feminist interventions, warning of their potential to unconsciously reproduce patriarchal logics. This tension is exemplified in debates surrounding Qasim Amin, often hailed as the progenitor of Arab feminism. Though his works (1899; 1900) called for reforms in polygamy and divorce laws, critics such as Ahmed (1992) argue that they served male interests under the guise of progress, and were deeply shaped by European liberal frameworks (El Guindi, 2003, 593).

Nonetheless, not all feminist perspectives frame the family solely as an oppressive construct. Hooks (1984, 37) points to its role as a kinship structure, wherein care and solidarity are practised—functions often eclipsed by critiques of sexism. The devaluation of family life in some feminist discourses, she argues, has reflected the positionality of bourgeois women who, unlike working-class counterparts, can opt out of familial care responsibilities through commodification (hooks, 1984, 39). This dynamic, she contends, alienated many women from feminist movements, even as feminism itself sought to transform familial relationships, not simply repudiate them.

Such transformations entail interrogating the ideological function of kinship. Mohanty (2003a, 57) insists that kinship structures must be examined as 'ideological practices', given their role in normalising gendered hierarchies. She critiques homogenising analyses that portray the patriarchal family as a universally shared cultural fixture, noting that such generalisations erase historical specificity and obscure power structures. For example, Minces' claim that Arab and Muslim societies share 'an almost identical vision of women' is problematised for its lack of reference to local histories, politics, and diverse interpretations of religious and legal texts (Mohanty, 2003a, 57). The mere description of marriage contracts, Mohanty notes, is often taken as evidence of women's subjugation without examining the broader socio-political context in which such contracts are embedded. Thus, feminist engagements with the family are not monolithic. While often depicted as a vehicle of patriarchal power, the family is also a terrain of contestation—its meanings and functions mutable, stratified, and deeply entangled with class, culture, and history.

Colonialism

The colonial encounter did not merely introduce secularism as a philosophical ideal; it reconstituted the political and legal landscape of colonised nations, embedding secular principles into state institutions in ways that altered perceptions of law, family, and gender. These transformations were not neutral; rather, they operated through hierarchies that empowered certain groups while disenfranchising others. This asymmetry emerged from a colonial logic that constructed the colonised subject as inferior, both morally and intellectually. Cohn (2013, 5) highlights how colonial authority was often justified through claims of racial inferiority; with Fanon (1963, 22) recalling how colonisers positioned themselves as the custodians of civilisation: 'on the other side of the ocean there was a race of less-than-humans who, thanks to us, might reach our status in a thousand years…' (Fanon, 1963, 22).

Yet, the colonial gaze was not evenly cast across territories. Fanon (1963) underscores the partial nature of colonial exploitation, observing that entire regions within a colonised country might remain untouched by direct intervention. This unevenness complicates any attempt to craft a unified narrative of colonial impact, prompting postcolonial theorists to challenge the universalised histories often written from a Western vantage point. Said's *Orientalism* (1978) does not simply expose orientalist fantasies; it reorients our attention towards how knowledge and space were wielded as instruments of power.

Within this epistemic and political order, gendered subjectivities were not exempt. The relationship between patriarchy and imperialism gave rise to specific portrayals of the 'Third World woman', positioned at the threshold of tradition and modernity—visible, yet voiceless. The absence of women in colonial histories is not incidental but structural. Kapur (2002, 9) invokes MacKinnon's claim that women everywhere experience subjugation under patriarchal power structures shaped by male law and justice. Yet this assertion flattens critical distinctions, neglecting how colonialism reshaped men's and women's lives in profoundly different ways, often subordinating both but in distinct registers.

The cultural production of the twentieth century—its literature, visual art, and social theory—bears the indelible mark of colonial entanglement. Hegde (1998, 281) points out that it is nearly impossible to understand this period without acknowledging how colonialism shaped aesthetic and ideological forms. New forms of resistance emerged in response, with nationalism fostering a 'critical consciousness' about the ongoing reach of Western influence. Yet this consciousness is not without tension. Jacobs (2003, 672) identifies the suspicion among women in postcolonial societies towards Western rhetoric on difference as justifiable. This wariness stems not from ignorance but from lived experience: the West's gaze often reduces non-Western women to archetypes—'victimized, tradition bound, and passive' (Hegde 1998, 281).

Despite the diversity of postcolonial experiences, many nations share a history shaped by colonisation, and this historical proximity allows for certain structural parallels. Rajan (1993, 6) notes that issues such as centralised state control, social inequality, the tension between nationalism and regionalism, and the dichotomy of 'tradition' and 'modernity' manifest in comparable ways across postcolonial contexts. These dynamics, in turn, influence how gender is constructed and contested.

These complexities are evident in the work of Qasim Amin, whose *The Liberation of Women* emerged from an intellectual milieu shaped by Islamic modernist thinkers such as Muhammad ʿAbduh and Jamal ad-Din al-Afghānī (Kurzman, 2002, 103). These figures argued that orthodox Islam lacked the conceptual tools to address modernity's challenges and sought reformist approaches that remained grounded in Islamic principles while engaging with rationalist discourse (Moaddel,

1998, 120). Amin's work, influenced by this intellectual tradition, constitutes one of the earliest sustained efforts to reconcile Islam with progressive views on gender (Moaddel 1998, 121). His writings sought not only to respond to Western critiques but to position Islam as a vehicle of reform and resistance against colonial hegemony.

Feminist theorists have since broadened the analytic lens to account for intersections of race and gender within colonial discourse. Mills (2005) traces how gender analysis became a necessary corrective to race-focused accounts, enabling deeper examinations of binaries within colonial power relations. Jayawardena (1986) similarly warns of how Western secular thought shaped institutions and ideas in ways that naturalised imperial authority. The dominance of such frameworks has led to increasing calls for the West to confront its own epistemic privileges. As Schutte (1998, 69) argues, decolonisation is not complete until the West learns to 'step out of its colonial boots' and recognise the structures it continues to impose. Yet even this gesture can be fraught. Sa'ar (2005) observes that feminism and secularism are often received in postcolonial contexts as foreign impositions, artefacts of imperialism cloaked in the language of liberation.

Secularism

The introduction of secularism, as understood within a broadly Western context, to Egypt and Iran was achieved via foreign powers (Egypt), and the desire to be viewed as a modern state (Iran). Western influences shaped each state's engagement, with models of *internal* and external secularism developing from this analysis and shaping our understanding of how it was introduced to each state (see also Cooke, 2021).

While Demerath (2007) uses these terms, his approach proposes four secularisation scenarios—'emergent', 'coercive', 'diffuse', and 'imperialist'—distinguished by directionality and agency. Internal secularism includes emergent forms, arising unintentionally from reforms in education or industry, and coercive forms, where top-down authority enforces secular norms (Demerath, 2007). External secularism, by contrast, includes diffuse models shaped by cultural interactions, and imperialist ones imposed by external actors (Demerath, 2007). Cooke (2019; 2021), however, departs from this framework identifying internal secularism in Iran as a consequence of Reza Khan's consolidation of power as *Šah* in 1925. Modernisation efforts were orchestrated by the state, with secularism flowing hierarchically through institutions—from central government to local authorities, and ultimately into public and private spheres such as education, commerce, and family life (Cooke, 2021).

By contrast, Egypt exemplifies external secularism, where imperial forces—directly or via policy—shaped the state's religious trajectory. This model mirrors internal secularism structurally, but here the colonial power assumes the role of primary decision-maker (Cooke, 2021). Imperial authority may interact with local rulers or bypass them entirely, embedding secular policy through administrative apparatuses that include localised colonial structures. These, too, trickle down into social institutions and households.

Crucially, Cooke's (2021) models provide broad frameworks to theorise top-down impositions of secularism while remaining open to bottom-up forces such as social movements. In doing so, they move beyond Demerath's (2007) typology by highlighting how authority—whether domestic or imperial—directly engineers secular stability in state formation. How we understand this, however, also directly relates to linguistic understandings and ambiguities.

The term *secular* branches into a constellation of related concepts—*secularisation*, *secularity*, and *secularism(s)*—whose frequent conflation in both scholarly and public discourse reveals a persistent lack of definitional precision (Fokas, 2010, 163). This conceptual ambiguity is not merely a matter of semantics; it reflects the shifting and context-dependent nature of the secular itself. Gellner (2001, 337) underscores the need for a 'contextualized and reflexive understanding', while Başkan (2014, 2) attributes the definitional instability to the elasticity of these terms and 'their indiscriminate application' across diverse domains. The term *secularisation*, for instance, has been invoked at multiple levels—individual, societal, organisational, public, political, and international—each carrying its own implications and assumptions (Başkan, 2014).

Rather than a linear decline in religiosity, secularisation signals a broader societal shift in which religious authority recedes and non-religious, or secular institutions and values gain prominence. Accordingly, secularisation is 'generally thought of as the name of some kind of decline of religion' (Taylor, 2007, 427).

Yet secularism is not merely a matter of institutional design. Rather, Agrama (2010, 502) argues that it is '...not a separation between religion and politics, but an *ongoing, deepening, entanglement in the question of religion and politics, for the purpose of identifying and securing fundamental liberal rights and freedoms*'. This tension underscores the conceptual fluidity of secularism, which, like religion, resists singular definition. To navigate this complexity, Kosmin (2007, 3) proposes a typology distinguishing between *hard* and *soft* secularism. The former, exemplified by regimes such as the former USSR and China, aligns closely with atheistic state ideologies. The latter, seen in countries like the UK, Denmark, and Israel, accommodates religion as a private matter while maintaining formal separation from religious institutions (Kosmin, 2007, 3, 7). Theocratic states such as contemporary Iran, by contrast, fall outside this secular spectrum altogether.

Within this context, Jackson (2024) challenges the overtly Western nature of secularism by deconstructing core concepts and providing a juristic lens which reflects the 'Islamic secular' rather than simply serving as a translation for a Western concept. While Jackson's (2024) is a key step in recognising alternative perspectives and applications, the Western lens is retained for this work due to the prominence of foreign influences in enforcing and influencing secularism's introduction to each state in the early twentieth century.

This lack of definitional cohesion becomes particularly salient when secularism is examined in the context of the MENA region. The Arabic term *'Ilmānīyah* (عِلْمانِيَّة; secularism),[2] introduced in the nineteenth century, marked the formal entry of secular discourse into the region (Najjar, 1996, 2; Badran, 2005, 10; Hashemi, 2010, 330). However, Arabic, Persian, and Turkish lack direct equivalents for the term *secularism*, a linguistic gap that reflects not incompatibility with Islamic thought but rather the semantic limitations of these languages. The Turkish term *laiklik*, derived from the French *laïcité*, illustrates this process of conceptual adaptation (Hashemi, 2010, 330).

Secularism's institutional manifestations vary widely. In some contexts, it has facilitated legal reforms impacting gender equality, particularly in matters of marriage and family law. Despite its conceptual ambiguities, secularism often functions as a vehicle for modernisation, predicated on the separation of religion from governance (Al-Ali, 2000). The divergent experiences of Egypt and Iran illustrate the multiplicity of secularising pathways, and thus the 'secular nature of the state', shaped by distinct political and historical conditions.

[2] There is no direct translation for 'secularism' in Arabic, with *'Ilmānīyah* meaning something similar to worldliness.

Diverging introductions of secularism in Egypt and Iran has resulted in the terms *'internal'* and *'external'* secularism being used in this book (see also Cooke, 2019 & 2021; Louden-Cooke, 2024). In Iran, secularisation unfolded as an *internally* driven project under *Reza Šah Pahlavi*, whose modernisation agenda foregrounded state-led reforms. Although foreign influences were present, the initiative was largely endogenous, building on earlier currents for an increasingly secular state from the *Qājār* (قاجار; Qajar) period and the Constitutional Revolution. Yet the reforms often prioritised symbolic over substantive change, revealing the limits of top-down secularisation.

Egypt's experience, by contrast, was shaped by *external* forces. Colonial authorities introduced secular principles into governance and legal frameworks, though their reach into everyday life remained limited. The contrast between Iran's internal and Egypt's external secularism highlights the diverse configurations of state power and their role in shaping secular outcomes.

Positioning Decisions

Exploring such complex, and often controversial, concepts which span history, brings to light issues of researcher positionality and the influences of personal and political beliefs. Becker (1967) highlights how we are often expected to take sides based on these beliefs, and how they can result in the 'deviant' being presented as bad and the other, 'morally correct', emerging as good. During this research I reflected on my beliefs about gender equality, family law, religion, and colonial history. This was based predominantly on understandings gained from readings, but also observations of different family dynamics and engagements with religion, and finally my observations and experiences as a white, agnostic, married woman living in the UK were reflected upon; with understandings of different experiences with gender discrimination and state environments developing from the literature and conversations.

As a white, agnostic, Western woman, I also have to be careful to not speak for 'participants' (Freire, 2000) or trying to elevate their position through this work (Bourke, 2014, 3). It is therefore through recognising my racial, gender, religious, and geographic positionalities that feminist debates are incorporated. These identity factors also serve to highlight criticisms that have emerged, some of the weaknesses of Western feminist theories become apparent, and thus speak to postcolonial feminist works.

Gender Equality, Matrimony and Secularism in Egypt and Iran therefore endeavours to be reflective in its approach, drawing on social, cultural, political, and legal components to create a framework within which interpretations of individual truths can be drawn, positioning the experiences of the individuals researched being central to my analysis.

The concept of truth speaks to Becker's (1967) observations on personal and political beliefs and essentially, the presence of unconscious bias in the research process as well as in the materials being used, and is again something I had to keep in mind. Truth is integral as 'It is important, then, to explore how reflexivity acts in the interests of "discourses of truth" (Pillow, 2003, 186) which "operate in relation to the dominant power structures of a given society"' (McNay, 1992, 25). D'Costa (2006, 132) posits that truth telling is perceived as necessary for the processes of 'peace-building, promoting democracy, striving for social justice, and transforming society more broadly', but questions 'whose truth is being told?'. However, a certain amount of scepticism has become pivotal in searching for the truth as it 'can encourage people to learn more and remain open to the possibility of their own errors' (Appleby et al., 2011, 7). The official mechanisms through which this truth is spoken is, however, frequently susceptible to manipulation by elites (D'Costa, 2006, 132), resulting in a selective truth being told. This speaks to the notion of relativism, whereby truth is 'relative to the position of the person making a statement' (Appleby et al., 2011, 7). This indicates that there is no whole truth, rather the subjective nature of experiences and the position of the researcher reinforces Appleby et al.'s (2011) assertion that no individual can be certain that their explanations are completely accurate, others must be listened to, and no one will have the final word on human histories. Subsequently, 'Telling the truth takes a collective effort' (Appleby et al., 1994, 309).

When examining countries such as those in the MENA region, colonial histories result in different truths emerging. A means of addressing the multifarious nature of 'truth', personal understanding and experiences can be utilised to reflect societal positioning and engagement with differing power structures. Ultimately, no single truth is obtainable. Rather, the intersecting nature of individual truths around similar experiences, alongside colonial 'truths', serves to reinforce the importance of identity and positionality in the recording of experiences and observations. Consequently, this book does not seek to provide a 'truth' about the effects of secularism on gender equality and marital rights; instead it seeks to provide a partial truth which will contribute to broader historical and contemporary puzzles about the point of contact between secularism, colonial powers, family law, and gender equality in Egypt and Iran and the effects resonating from it.

Within the context of existing debates on representations, the use of Western theories and debates, such as those of feminism and secularism, may be questioned. This is partly due to my positionality. Research 'represents a shared space' which is affected by our perceptions of others and 'the ways in which we expect others will perceive us' (Bourke, 2014, 1) and 'within positionality theory, it is acknowledged that people have multiple overlapping identities. Thus people make meaning from various aspects of their identity…' (Kezar, 2002, 96). It is here that concepts such as orientalism and islamophobia emerge as pivotal when considering my engagements with this research. Critical interactions with such prominent topics highlight the importance of reflexivity between myself as researcher, and those whose experiences I am drawing on. Orientalist critiques of homogenising representations, amalgamating experiences and 'mirroring' Western behaviours onto non-Western individuals, must therefore be recognised in my engagements. In order to recognise positionality and potential biases during the research process, reflexivity must occur. This involves the researcher engaging in 'self-scrutiny' (Bourke, 2014, 2) which results in 'increased attention to researcher subjectivity in the research process' and recognition of how the role of personal understanding of the 'self' impacts data collection and the acquisition of knowledge (Pillow, 2003, 176). A primary tenet of postcolonial theory is recognising truths and voices that are not those of white, western colonial victors. Through recognising my identity and positionality in relation to this research, it became possible for a more reflexive and critical relationship to occur between myself and the sources I engage with.

Another component I had to consider was the use of the term 'feminism'. Al-Ali (2000, 4) justifies her use of the term 'women's activism' rather than 'feminism' due to her interviewees 'pragmatic and ideological' rejection of the term. The attribution of the terms 'feminist' and 'feminism' to individuals, groups, and activities examined may not accurately represent their (intended) identities. While 'feminism' and 'feminist' will be used, this is primarily due to the inclusion of feminist theory and the apparent absence of refutation to the application of these terms. This silence, however, does not represent acceptance of the term as a form of identity.

In addition to my own positionality, the identities of those whose experiences are explored was a key area for consideration. Literacy, social or political prominence, and class are all to be reflected upon when engaging with personal accounts, with many individuals not recording their experiences or archival weeding resulting in accounts not being kept. Although I engaged with 'participant absent' research (Grant, 2018), the use of personal accounts brings individual experiences to the fore of this research, along with official documents. Analysis of these documents thus brought to light insights about individuals diverging interactions with these power structures, utilising language and experience to understand perspectives of and experiences with secularism, family law, and colonialism in relation to gendered restrictions.

Returning to Power Structures

Uniting these power structures is patriarchy, which in itself is a power formation. Addressing this, Bethke Elshtain (1981, 212) articulates the importance of remembering that the historic, patriarchal way of life was 'a precapitalist social form'. Connell (1987, 130) magnifies this by stipulating that the patriarchal state can be viewed as the outcome of 'a reverberating set of power relations and political processes in which patriarchy is both constructed and contested'; reinforcing the historical direction of the state as pivotal in comprehending its role in sexual politics.

Understandings of patriarchy have altered over time and this is evidenced by Weber's (1947) adoption of the term to refer to a 'system of government in which men ruled societies through their position as heads of households' (Walby, 1989, 214). In Islam, the importance and integrity of the family has been stressed (Eshkevari, 2013, 195), with arguments that the 'archaic traditions' which are practised not being able to 'have a reasonable Islamic defence' as they are incompatible with 'neither our theological and epistemological assumptions nor contemporary notions of justice'. This is emphasised through the pyramid structuring of seventh-century Arabian families with men at the top, highlighting how rights were 'naturally assigned' based on 'the patriarchal ethos on which social order was based' (Eshkevari, 2013, 195). Arguing in favour of the need for laws and regulations for the family, the notion of recognising the family as a 'joint enterprise' is put forward, whereby no member has superiority based on natural rights; rather rights of familial members should be determined by 'what is accepted as good practice in our time…' and in accordance 'with a definition of justice that is both local and contemporary' (Eshkevari, 2013, 196).

The issue of patriarchy has been a constant concern throughout twentieth-century Egypt and Iran, and has continued into the twenty-first century. Within the Egyptian context, such concerns became increasingly prominent during times of revolution 'whether masculinist power over women, or the power of one class over the other, or one generation over the other, and with that pinnacle of patriarchal power, the state' (Badran, 2014, 48). This is evidenced through the need to understand the historical context surrounding the importance of sexual morality and gendered behaviour (De Groot, 1996, 41). Iran illustrates this as they were placed on the 'political/ideological agenda' following events such as the Constitutional Revolution, social movements in the 1940s and the establishment of the Islamic Republic of Iran (IRI) in 1979. Similar observations can be made in Egypt, with the concerns which have been articulated serving different purposes within both states, with some seeking to reinforce more traditional frameworks within which women operate, and others seeking to further enable female participation and choice in society.

This is reinforced by arguments that gender politics of the IRI may be 'characterized as sometimes erratic and confounding, appearing to take one step forward and two steps back' (Moghadam, 2013, 206). This is evidenced through Khomeini's issuing of fatvā (فتوا; religious rulings) which would permit female divorce and encouraged them to include stipulations in the marriage contract (Moghadam, 2013, 206). Throughout the 1990s amendments to family law following advocacy of women's rights occurred under Presidents Rafsanjani and Khatami (Moghadam, 2013, 206). Similarly, amendments to Egyptian family laws in 1979 granted women the right to divorce should polygamy occur, however, in 1985, this was reversed and women lost their automatic right to divorce in this situation. In both instances, the prominence of the patriarchal power structure emerges, reinforcing fluctuations in the patriarchal nature of the legal and domestic frameworks within which women operate.

In this context, patriarchal systems have often been interpreted through universalist or essentialist frameworks. For instance, Eisenstein (1979) conceptualised patriarchy primarily as a biological expression of maleness. Yet, as Lazreg (1994, 54) notes, such approaches tend to treat patriarchy as an ahistorical and static construct, thereby contributing to the persistent generalisation of women's historical experiences. This work, *Gender Equality, Matrimony, and Secularism in Egypt and Iran*, aims to disrupt such tendencies by foregrounding individual narratives and context-specific engagements with intersecting power structures, offering a textured account grounded in personal histories and critical reflection.

As previously shown, power structures are not neatly confined to the public realm; they extend deeply into the private, particularly through the family, which emerges as a site of negotiation and contestation across geographic and cultural boundaries. Within familial spaces, dynamics of responsibility, authority, and labour division come to the fore. However, privileging one generation's feminist framework over another—as often happens through the metaphor of feminist 'waves'—risks replicating the masculinist hierarchies inherent in the familial structure and obscuring intergenerational complexities (Gillis et al. 2007, xxvi). To counter this, feminist historiography must foster intergenerational dialogues that avoid reductive periodisation and acknowledges shifting responsibilities and solidarities across time.

Spivak's seminal question—*Can the Subaltern Speak?*—remains a crucial touchstone for addressing the enduring tension between the 'necessities of historical and political representation' and the forms of subaltern existence that elude institutional mechanisms of voice and visibility (Birla 2010, 98). Within this framework, the interrelated power structures explored throughout this book do not aim to present a totalising narrative, but instead offer a provisional map of historic agency and discursive formation. Such a map facilitates a more nuanced comprehension of the conditions that continue to shape women's lives and legal status in contemporary Egypt and Iran—recognising that our understanding will always be more, but never fully, complete.

Moving Forward

This chapter has woven together a network of complex themes that converge at the intersection of individual agency and state authority. By interrogating patriarchal structures and the persistent entanglement of religion and family law within the framework of *Sharīʿah*, it becomes evident that expanding our understanding of the relationship between secularism, gender equality, and family law in Egypt and Iran is both necessary and urgent. Rather than dismissing these states as inherently incompatible with secularism, this book argues that the fault lies in the nature of the secular models adopted—often externally imposed, inconsistently applied, or co-opted by nationalist projects. Through the lived experiences of individuals, legislative developments, and colonial discourses, it becomes clear that the codification of family law in the early twentieth century was both a response to European imperial interventions and a strategic effort by local elites to modernise on their own terms. In this climate, the reconfiguration of the public/private divide opened both new arenas of possibility and entrenched sites of constraint for women challenging patriarchal power, whether rooted in the colonial state, the family, or both. By tracking the effects of secular statehood on women's legal rights within family structures, and how these affected both men and women, the book reveals the continued relevance of these dynamics into the twenty-first century.

The analysis focuses on dominant power structures in early twentieth-century Egypt and Iran—structures which, though transformed, persist in contemporary forms. Over a two-year period, archival research was undertaken to examine colonial documents, translated constitutions, and press materials, focusing particularly on how legal and political shifts were articulated and understood by colonial powers and domestic actors. This inquiry extended to autobiographies and memoirs of pivotal figures, analysed through a postcolonial feminist framework attentive to the layering of identities and the hierarchies that shaped them. Language—its deployment in governance, personal narrative, and public discourse—emerged as both a mechanism of control and a site of resistance.

Having laid the foundation in this chapter by situating key power structures within historical and theoretical frameworks, and by reflecting on the author's own positionality as a Western scholar engaging with non-Western histories, the book transitions in Chapter 2 to a focused examination of family law. The chapter uses the legal processes of marriage formation and dissolution to explore how secularism and political modernity reshaped gender norms in both states. Chapter 3 broadens the scope, turning to moments of upheaval—conflicts, revolutions, and constitutional reform—to demonstrate how colonial and imperial legacies constrained or enabled personal and collective agency. These disruptions are shown to be deeply embedded in the evolution of family law and reveal secularism's dual role as both an instrument of state control and a potential strategy for resistance.

Chapters 4 and 5 delve into the specific legal and experiential dimensions of marriage and divorce, drawing upon personal testimonies and statutory texts to illuminate the lived realities behind legal doctrines. Through the lens of individual narratives—reflections on *mahr*, legal barriers, and reformist aspirations—emerges a portrait of activism that does not seek to reject Islamic but rather pursues interpretive flexibility and greater autonomy. These chapters position such figures not as antagonists of religious tradition, but as interlocutors engaging critically with its constraints.

The final chapter synthesises the findings by drawing together the legal rights and restrictions experienced by men and women across both states, highlighting the nuanced impact of secular reforms on gender equality. Attention is given to the linguistic shifts within legal documents, the resonances of these shifts in public discourse, and the interplay between domestic gender movements and Western ideological influences. The central conclusion underscores that the secular orientation of the state did influence gender dynamics in family law—not through wholesale transformation, but through specific legal and rhetorical interventions that shaped the contours of equality and resistance in both Egypt and Iran.

Gender Equality, Modernity, and the State

Family law and matters of personal status, firmly situated within the religious jurisdiction of *Sharīʿah*, have long constituted sites of both domestic and international contestation. As the primary unit in which individuals are physically and morally reproduced, the family structure functions not only as a social institution but also as a key mechanism for reinforcing patriarchal gender hierarchies (Moghadam, 2013). It delineates the acceptable boundaries of sexual conduct and legitimises filiation, thereby maintaining established social orders through marital alliances and the regulation of kinship (Dunne, 1998). Despite frequent assumptions that colonial authorities were reluctant to intervene in family law due to its perceived centrality to religious doctrine and communal identity (Asad, 2003), the very framing of *Sharīʿah* as synonymous with personal status law reflects a deeper secular logic.

Asad (2003) argues that this translation of *Sharīʿah* into a discrete domain of family law was part of a broader secular project—one that effectively privatised religion and restructured it in a manner conducive to the formation of self-governing, modern subjects. By codifying *Sharīʿah* in this way, colonial and postcolonial legal regimes simultaneously preserved the symbolic role of religion while delimiting its scope, thereby depoliticising it and reducing it to a system governing intimate relations. The reconfiguration of *Sharīʿah* as a fixed body of family law

S. Louden-Cooke, *Gender Equality, Matrimony and Secularism in Egypt and Iran: A Comparative Exploration of Early Twentieth-Century Family Law*, Middle East Today,
https://doi.org/10.1007/978-3-032-00846-6_2

can thus be seen not as a preservation of religious authenticity, but as a product of secular rationality embedded in modern statecraft (Asad, 2003).

Family law occupies a pivotal space in legal systems across the MENA region, acting not merely as a repository of personal status regulations, but as a site where state authority and religious legitimacy intersect. With the exception of Tunisia and Turkey, where codified civil law has replaced clerical authority in matters of marriage, divorce, and inheritance, most MENA states continue to delegate personal status law to officially recognised religious bodies (Joseph, 1996). This delegation visibly reinforces male-dominated hierarchies, with the daily application of these laws makes evident how patriarchal control is not only preserved but ritualised through legal practice, embedded in seemingly routine judicial and familial procedures.

Qutb (2001), known for his stringent Qur'anic hermeneutics, positions the family as the divine scaffold of society, formed through the spiritual union of complementary souls. Yet his assertions that Islam elevates women 'to a position of dignity' sit uneasily against a backdrop of family law practices widely criticised for gender inequality (Qutb, 2001: 25).

Acknowledging Egyptian developments in 2004 which granted women more rights in divorce, the continued prevalence of gender discrimination are highlighted (Nazir, 2005). Abu-Odeh (2004: 1049), however, recognises interpretational differentials between schools of thought and reform potential by way of a spectrum. She (2004) argues that Tunisian legislative reform presents itself as the most liberal, with *Hanafī*, which Lombardi (1998: 94) notes 'claims the nominal allegiance' of sixty per cent of the world's Muslims—including the majority of Egyptians, and upon which Egyptian family law is based—being the most conservative (Abu-Odeh, 2004). Despite *Hanafī*'s strictly conservative nature, Egypt is situated centrally on the spectrum representing 'centrist reforms' (Abu-Odeh, 2004: 1049). Moreover, Egyptian family law reforms preserved gender reciprocity as inherited from Taqlid[1] law

[1] Taqlid law is inherited from the 'pre-modern Islamic legal system. With regard to marriage, both Taqlid law and general Islamic law stipulate that women 'retain both their juridical personality as well as whatever property they own when they enter marriage'. Additionally, they are not required to 'maintain the marital household except under limited circumstances when the husband is in need'. These rules defined the manner in which the family was expected to operate, and their significance not only assists in further

while simultaneously chipping away at the husband's 'surplus powers in the family' (Abu Oden, 2004: 1049).

Within the Iranian household, one perception of its re-Islamisation following the demise of the *Šah* (شاه; King) was that safeguarding the family 'required the strengthening of male privilege', with the Family Protection Law being replaced with the reinstated 1936 Civil Code (Paidar, 1996: 58–59). This reversion is understood to have revoked rights afforded to women in areas such as abortion, divorce, marriage, and child custody, almost instantaneously. Additionally, compulsory hijab and extensive gender segregation were implemented, alongside methods for regulating family integrity. These policies fell under the umbrella of the 'anti-corruption crusade' (Paidar, 1996: 59). Moreover, the reestablishment of a rigid public/private dichotomy reinforced gender differences and the regulating of family integrity contributing towards politicising the private sphere.

The most far-reaching effects of the later revoked Iranian Family Protection Law was increasing marriage ages to eighteen and twenty for women and men respectively (Higgins, 1985: 480). The ease of male divorce was mired by the compulsory use of a court rather than simply declaring divorce with two witnesses (Higgins, 1985: 480). The grounds for female divorce were broadened and they were permitted to seek custody of children; however, to women's detriment, the revocation of the law resulted in lowering marriage age to thirteen. It also resulted in increased constrictions to female divorce and greater ease of male divorce, with comprehensive reforms of family law being unlikely due to the continued reliance on *Sharī'ah* (Higgins, 1985: 480–481). Subsequently, fluctuations are demonstrated in the liberal nature of state policies in very specific areas of family law. While the pre-revolution era was shaped by rigid policies of secularism and state modernisation, family law remained virtually untouched, with state power over the private sphere being ensured. These divergences point to unresolved silences regarding how gender-egalitarian reforms contribute to state legitimacy, and the extent to which external actors shape their implementation.

understanding historical patriarchal relations, but also contemporary family legal dynamics as they 'are the precursor to family law in the Arab world (Abu-Odeh, 2004: 1051; 1062–1063; 1067).

Marriage

The regulation of marriage—its establishment and dissolution—constitutes one of the most gender-salient areas of Islamic law (Mir-Hosseini, 2009). As such, marital rights offer a compelling lens through which to assess the broader societal status of women (Engineer, 2008). In many societies and religious traditions, women's autonomy in choosing a marital partner has historically been curtailed, grounded in patriarchal assumptions about their supposed emotional or intellectual inferiority. This dominant perception, however, is contested by *Sūrah* (سُورَة; chapter) 33:35, which affirms the moral and spiritual parity of men and women in the eyes of God (Pickthall, 2012; Ahmed, 1992; Engineer, 2008). The verse explicitly enumerates qualities—such as devotion, piety, and truthfulness—as equally applicable to both sexes, thereby providing scriptural grounding for gender equality in matters of personal status.

From an Islamic ethical standpoint, marriage is envisioned not merely as a lawful arrangement for sexual relations but as the moral cornerstone of family life and, by extension, social stability. Engineer (2008) characterises it as a union predicated on dignity, trust, and mutual respect, designed to safeguard the spiritual and material well-being of both spouses. Marriage is thus interpreted as both a personal and societal obligation, underscored by the Prophet Muhammad's assertion that 'marriage is half of religion', (Eaton, 1994: 188) a statement often cited to elevate its religious and social significance.

Eaton (1994: 188) deepens this analysis by portraying marriage as the nexus through which individual strands of social relations are interwoven into the broader communal fabric. In his analogy of the 'great web of relationships', marriage acts as both the structural anchor and ethical conduit of the Islamic community. Yet, while Eaton's emphasis on the social cohesion facilitated by marriage offers a holistic view of its communal function, his subsequent endorsement of polygamy as a legitimate extension of family life reveals underlying tensions. He contends that polygamous arrangements help maintain the continuity of this social web, portraying them as 'complementary to the close-knit communal life of the city' (Eaton, 1994: 189). This rationale, however, raises questions regarding gender equity, as it normalises a practice that structurally privileges male agency in forming multiple marital ties, while limiting reciprocal autonomy for women.

Engineer (2008: 187) observes that polygamy in Islam is 'contextual whereas monogamy is normative', highlighting that polygamy was historically sanctioned under specific conditions—namely, to ensure the welfare of widows and orphans in wartime—rather than as a generalised marital ideal. Across the MENA region, state responses to polygamy have oscillated between restriction and prohibition, shaped by political ideologies and the tension between religious doctrine and evolving conceptions of women's rights. These varying approaches reflect how legal reform on polygamy often becomes a proxy for broader societal debates on modernity, religious authority, and women's status in the public and private spheres.

In contrast to its prevalence across much of the MENA region, polygamy was rare in Iran, with data from 1966 showing that only around one per cent of men were in polygamous unions (Higgins, 1985). Islam's arrival curtailed the pre-Islamic practice of unlimited wives, restricting men to four and setting conditions such as financial capacity and equitable treatment of all spouses (Qutb, 2001). Rather than abolishing polygamy outright, Islam regulated it, justifying its continued existence as a pragmatic response to the complexities of human nature and social needs (Qutb, 2001). However, there is a contested narrative about whether early Islam marked a regression or advancement in women's rights. While Ahmed (1992: 37) argues that some women in pre-Islamic Arabia enjoyed greater freedoms, orthodox interpretations of Islam rigidified gender roles by rendering Muhammad's practices and regulations universally binding. This contrasts with more reformist or context-sensitive interpretations that emphasised the ethical essence of Islam and its adaptability to evolving social conditions (Ahmed, 1992: 58).

Variations in marital rights across Islamic regions further complicate the historical narrative. Women in Medina were not permitted to contract their own marriages, while in Kufa they could do so without a male guardian (Ahmed, 1992: 59), reflecting how geography and legal schools shaped gender norms. Similarly, Karmi (2005: 173) notes that pre-Islamic women often remained within their kinship networks after marriage, with their husbands—if not kin—visiting them, a pattern reflecting both independence and flexibility. While Stern (cited in Karmi, 2005: 173) suggests polygamy was rare or even absent in this period, it may have been masked by the use of *sigheh*. Additionally, polyandry and immediate remarriage after divorce were not uncommon (Karmi, 2005:

172–173), further challenging contemporary assumptions about gender and family in early Arab societies. The relative autonomy of women during this time can be partially attributed to the prominence of notable women in Islamic history and the tension between matrilineal and patrilineal social systems from which Islam emerged (Karmi, 2005: 173).

Another contentious dimension of Islamic marital law is the age of marriage, particularly child marriage. Classical patriarchal interpretations often placed girls in the households of their husbands' families, where they were subordinate not only to men but also to older women (Kandiyoti, 1991: 31). By the early twentieth century, figures like Malak Hifni Nasif in Egypt had begun publicly critiquing this practice, identifying its harmful consequences for women's health and well-being (Baron, 1991: 281). In Iran, child marriage persisted particularly in rural, impoverished areas, where economic precarity, environmental stressors such as drought, and the social utility of consolidating kinship ties served to reinforce early marriage. Notably, religion appeared to play a diminishing role in the motivation for such unions, supplanted instead by material and social considerations (Bahramitash & Kazemipour, 2006: 113).

Divorce

Emerging alongside marriage—long situated within patriarchal social and legal frameworks—is the institution of divorce. Traditionally, men held the unilateral right to initiate divorce, often by invoking *ṭalāq* (طَلَاق; proclamation of divorce), which could be pronounced within specific contextual conditions (Abu-Odeh, 2004; Strong, 1997). During the *al-'Iddah* (الْعِدَّة; waiting period), a wife is required to remain in her husband's home, with the husband maintaining financial responsibility until the period ends. Upon finalisation, financial obligations generally cease unless the couple shares children, in which case the father remains responsible until custody transitions (Abu-Odeh, 2004).

Despite the Islamic ideal that divorce should be discouraged due to its potentially destabilising social and emotional effects (Engineer, 2008), empirical data points to its growing prevalence. In Iran, divorce declined in the 1980s and 1990s but had risen again by the early 2000s; by 2001, roughly 10 per cent of marriages ended in divorce, with 1.9 per cent of women aged 30–34 recorded as divorced in 2002 (Bahramitash & Kazemipour, 2006: 123). Paradoxically, in Iraq, divorce was weaponised by the Ba'athist regime as a political tool during and after the Iran-Iraq

War. The government offered financial incentives to men willing to divorce Iranian wives, while encouraging women to leave husbands suspected of evading military service, holding foreign citizenship, or residing abroad for extended periods (Efrati, 2005).

In Iran, debates over the ease of male-initiated divorce contributed to increased divorce rates during the 1980s (Keddie, 2001: 6), which appears to contradict earlier claims of its decline (Bahramitash & Kazemipour, 2006: 123). Legal reforms followed this public concern: in 1989, all divorces were required to obtain court approval before registration, and in 1994, a set of twelve justifications were granted to women seeking divorce, alongside increased financial burdens on men (Keddie, 2001: 6–7). However, geographic and socio-economic disparities remained; urban women were significantly more likely to access these legal reforms than their rural or tribal counterparts (Higgins, 1985: 485).

Notably, Egypt's Law 100/1985 marked a progressive turn by allowing women to obtain a divorce on the basis of insistence alone, even in the absence of demonstrable harm. This reform arguably brought Egyptian women close to achieving access to a form of no-fault divorce, reflecting a rare convergence of religious accommodation and gender-equalising reform (Abu-Odeh, 2004). While significant legal asymmetries persist across the MENA region, the evolution of divorce laws reveals complex intersections of religion, politics, and gendered legal subjectivity.

Inheritance and Child Custody

Other critical domains of family law where gender inequality remains pronounced are inheritance and child custody. Pre-Islamic norms largely excluded women from inheritance (Qutb, 2001: 44). With the advent of Islam, however, a framework was introduced that entitled all relatives to inherit based on their degree of kinship to the deceased (Qutb, 2001: 46). Still, inequality persisted: a husband may inherit half of his wife's estate, while a wife receives only one-quarter of her husband's, and this share is further reduced if (grand)children are involved (Qutb, 2001: 56–57).

In Iran, gender hierarchies govern custodial rights, with paternal custody automatically granted once children reach a certain age (Strong, 1997). Yet, the rigidity of this arrangement was temporarily relaxed during the Iran-Iraq War, when widespread widowhood led Ayatollah

Khomeini to permit women custody of their children—an unprecedented departure from traditional *Sharīʿah* norms (Keddie, 2001). This pragmatic exception illustrates how political crises can prompt short-term reform, though such changes do not necessarily alter the underlying patriarchal foundations of family law.

While Iran acknowledged the impact of war on custody, it remains unclear whether Iraq responded similarly despite sharing comparable conditions. Family law continues to operate within the religiously governed private sphere, while the public sphere experiences more overt secularisation. This divide reflects a broader structural inconsistency in state approaches to gender equality, sustaining gender segregation and impeding comprehensive reform.

Dividing the State

State structuring has historically relied on the division between public and private spheres, with family law firmly embedded within the latter. In medieval Islamic societies, sex was regarded as inescapable and omnipresent, with the public/private divide functioning as a mechanism to preserve social order by reinforcing binary gender roles and legitimising unequal rights (Entelis, 1996; Sanders, 1991). Although interaction between unrelated men and women was acknowledged as inevitable, strict gender segregation was instituted to ensure that such interactions remained licit—most commonly through marriage (Sanders, 1991). Alternatively, *zinā* (زِنَا; illicit sexual relations), constituted the clearest violation of this order. Jurists often framed women as the primary instigators of *fitnah* (فِتْنَة; temptation), due to their perceived potential to engage in unlawful sexual conduct with men (Sanders, 1991).

Within this framework, the public/private dichotomy emerges not only as a structural division but also as a form of gendered social control. Women's relegation to the private sphere was portrayed as a protective measure aimed at preserving their honour, yet this justification implicitly cast women as morally suspect in public settings. Two central issues arise here: first, the assumption that women are inherently untrustworthy in the public domain; and second, the application of a gendered lens to moral transgressions, wherein male participation in *zinā* is relatively unproblematised. Thus, rather than offering true protection, the dichotomy reinforces gender hierarchies and entrenches behavioural stereotypes that legitimise the subordination of women.

Mernissi (cited in Lewis & Mills, 2003: 15) characterises this divide as both an ideological and experiential cleavage in Muslim society—between the male space of the *ummāh* (أُمَّة; community) and the domestic, female space of the family. In this context, the *ḥijāb* (الحجاب; veil) functions as a symbolic and practical tool for maintaining this boundary. It allows women to navigate public space while ostensibly retaining the protective seclusion of the private sphere, thereby safeguarding both their honour and societal order from the perceived chaos of *fitnah* (Lewis & Mills, 2003). While this interpretation presents the veil as a mechanism of mutual protection, it also perpetuates deeply rooted assumptions about women's inherent capacity to disrupt public order. Consequently, the veil becomes a material expression of the dichotomy, simultaneously embodying and reinforcing gendered behavioural expectations.

Within the colonial context, the 'discourse of uplifting an entire population onto a higher plane of material and moral well-being' was intricately linked to representations of gender and segregation (Shakry, 1998: 128). Within this framework, the image of the secluded woman became a symbol of societal 'backwardness', prompting colonial policies to intervene in, and ultimately attempt to restructure, the private sphere (Shakry, 1998: 128). This illustrates how colonialism contributed to the reinforcement—and reconfiguration—of the public/private dichotomy. Shakry (1998) furthers this argument by highlighting that the efficacy of colonial interventions was contingent upon their capacity to access and reshape the private domain. The colonial restructuring of this dichotomy functioned as a *conceptual tool for ordering society*, allowing colonial powers to regulate both social and personal realms while establishing a secular public sphere suitable for governance (Hafez, 2011). Mitchell (1991) critiques normalising this binary by conceptualising the state as 'an effect' rather than 'a separate entity', thereby encouraging a more nuanced understanding of how social processes and power structures are reproduced within the framework of state authority (Hafez, 2011: 16).

Critiques of the modern, Western liberal public sphere further complicate this analysis. Although Habermas (1962/1989: 27) championed the bourgeois public sphere as a critical space for rational discourse among private individuals acting as a public, scholars such as Ryan (1992) and Eley (1992) (cited in Asad 2003: 183), underscore its exclusionary nature. They contend that the Western liberal public sphere historically marginalised women, the propertyless, and religious minorities. Susen (2011: 43) advances this critique by arguing that the public sphere, though 'composed of private individuals', is not neatly separated from their personal lives. Rather, 'every public persona is embedded in the background subjectivity of a private person', revealing the permeability of the public/private divide. Moreover, Susen (2011) proposes that these realms are mutually constitutive, not mutually exclusive, with their interaction shaping the social fabric. The Western roots of this sphere are hugely problematic when blue-printing such concepts onto other societies, with states within areas such as the MENA region requiring their own equivalents which may not reflect Western models.

Eickelman and Salvatore (2002: 94) expand this discussion by reorienting the public sphere as the site of contestation over definitions of the 'common good', encompassing moral values, civic obligations, and societal rights. They criticise Habermas' early work for overlooking religion's centrality in many societies (Eickelman & Salvatore, 2002: 96). In contexts where religious expression is regulated—such as secular Turkey or Baʿthist Syria—religious practice remains fundamental to public identity and meaning-making (Eickelman & Salvatore, 2002: 102). The emergence of the Muslim Brotherhood in the 1920s exemplifies the integration of religious practice into the public sphere, with such groups adapting to play politically and socially influential roles in their respective public spheres (Eickelman & Salvatore, 2002).

Consequently, identity in these societies is not merely political but deeply rooted in religious tradition. The 'Muslim public', therefore, is best understood as a product of evolving practices that integrate Islamic traditions with modern social life, thereby challenging both secular and liberal conceptualisations of public space (Eickelman & Salvatore, 2002: 112).

The exclusionary public sphere is thus presented as

> a space *necessarily* (not just contingently) articulated by power. And everyone who enters it must address power's disposition of people and things, the dependence of some on the goodwill of others.
>
> (Asad, 2003: 184)

Moreover, the secularist apprehension surrounding religion's influence on personal choice has been challenged, in part due to the restrictive and authoritative nature of many religious prescriptions (Asad, 2003: 185–186). In seeking to move beyond Western conceptualisations of the public sphere, Thompson redefines it as a '*civic order*'—a term that underscores the intersection of civic participation with broader structural forces (Landes, 2003: 29). She also highlights the importance of integrating economic systems alongside state structures as a means of reimagining the formulation of both public and private realms (Landes, 2003: 29).

This perspective is echoed by Olsen (1993: 158), who introduces a second axis of public/private division: the market/family binary, which she deems particularly consequential for women. However, the parallel drawn between market and family provoked critique from Locke, who perceived the family as inherently unequal—rooted in the hierarchical parent–child relationship—while the market was to be governed by equality among individuals (Eisenstein, 1981: 39). Locke's resistance to equating the family with political society can be interpreted in two ways. First, the concept of public equality cannot be transposed onto the private realm because of its hierarchical structure. Second, blurring these spheres risks unsettling established boundaries, potentially allowing women's entrance into the economic domain and thereby challenging the privileged status of the political over the domestic. This reveals how the political sphere was historically positioned as superior to the familial, thus reinforcing the hierarchical structure of social realms. As will be shown in the context of Egyptian and Iranian family law, even when these spheres are not formally paralleled, they do converge in practice. Locke's distinction thereby serves as a useful analytical lens through which to understand patriarchal family hierarchies within the broader framework of state authority; especially within the colonial context.

While debates continue regarding whether the public/private dichotomy supports or disrupts religious moral authority, this book focuses on how a predominantly public concept—secularism—interacts with and influences a domain traditionally located within the private sphere: the family. As the boundaries between these realms increasingly blur, it becomes possible to critically examine how modern secular governance impacts religious family law and the extent to which it alters, reinforces, or subverts gendered power relations within that legal framework.

Feminism and Modernity

Modernity is commonly understood as emerging from a cultural framework characterised by 'stability, coherence, discipline and world-mastery', and is thus often equated with ideals of progress, reason, and democracy (Felski, 1995: 11). Its association with masculinity is not a recent development; rather, the institutional structures of the nineteenth century—particularly the public sphere—are considered central to this gendered identification, effectively positioning women outside of public and political life (Felski, 1995: 16). This framing underscores the paradoxical nature of modernity: while it purported to herald a new era of universal emancipation, it simultaneously entrenched the exclusion and subordination of women (Werbner & Yuval-Davis, 1999: 6). The legacy of modernity in the MENA region is further complicated by the rise of authoritarian regimes in the wake of colonial rule, with Hallaq (2005: 206) arguing that this phenomenon represents one of the 'tragic results' of modernity's violent imposition on long-standing cultural and religious traditions. However, what remains ambiguous is the referent of 'modernity' in these critiques—whether it denotes secularisation policies, state-building efforts, or the colonial imposition of alien norms and traditions alongside other modernising reforms. This raises the question of whether modernity itself is inherently problematic, or whether its destructiveness lies in the manner and context of its implementation.

Within these broader debates, the notion of political modernity emerges as a significant concept. It is this strand that Chakrabarty (2000: 20) attempts to reconceptualise within a non-Western context, with the aim of interrogating both the applicability and limitations of European-derived social and political categories. European intellectual influence has become so deeply embedded globally that, as Chakrabarty (2000: 4) notes, 'it is impossible to think of anywhere in the world without invoking certain categories and concepts', all of which are fundamentally rooted in European historical experience. Political modernity, therefore, is inseparable from the legacies of the Enlightenment and the nineteenth century, given its intrinsic association with key concepts such as citizenship, the public sphere, and the public/private dichotomy (Chakrabarty, 2000). These concepts continue to shape institutional frameworks and cultural imaginaries globally, often obscuring the historical contingencies and cultural particularities that challenge their presumed universality.

Colonialism emerges as a key vehicle through which constructions of modernity and European thought were disseminated throughout the non-Western world. It introduced 'many of the desires and institutions of European bourgeois modernity but without, it would seem, the family romance of bourgeois Europe' (Chakrabarty, 2000: 216). However, Chakrabarty (2000) critiques the construction of Europe as a mythical and singular origin of modernity, particularly when employed as a reference point for evaluating capitalist transitions in non-Western contexts.

Such comparisons reinforce the notion of incomplete or 'unfinished' modernity in these regions. As a corrective, Chakrabarty (2000) argues for recognising this process not as direct conversion but as *translation*, where modernity is reinterpreted within specific cultural and historical contexts.

Critiques of modernity extend beyond economic and political spheres to its relationship with the Enlightenment. Feminist scholars have long problematised Enlightenment ideals for their internal contradictions, especially concerning gender (Moghissi, 1999: 78). While it purported to champion individual freedoms, these freedoms were granted in accordance with the state's understanding of the 'individual'—a construct implicitly male. Consequently, modernity has often served to liberate men while reinforcing constraints on women (Moghissi, 1999: 78–79). Postmodernist critiques contend that the Enlightenment merely substituted older typologies with new dichotomies, leaving underlying hierarchies intact. Within the MENA region, as Moghissi (1999: 83) notes, modernisation over the last century has frequently failed to enact genuinely transformative reforms in gender equality.

The paradox of the Enlightenment is further reflected in its influence on and opposition to Western feminism. The male-dominated intellectual tradition of the Enlightenment has been a central target of feminist critique, as women struggled for recognition within frameworks that prized rationality and objectivity—qualities historically aligned with masculinity (Ramazanoğlu, 2002: 24). This critique extends to colonial assumptions of Western superiority, where Enlightenment thinkers associated the West with epistemic authority over natural and social truths (Ramazanoğlu, 2002: 25). Yeğenoğlu (1998: 95–96) refers to this as the imposition of 'one history', where non-Western societies are measured against a singular Western timeline of progress.

While scholars such as Badran (2007) and Mernissi (1991) have explored productive intersections between Islam and feminism, and Al-Ali (2000) has reconceptualised secularism in the Egyptian women's movement, both secularism and feminism are still often viewed as Western impositions. Jayawardena's (1986) documentation of feminist movements in non-Western contexts highlights their diverse origins, yet this recognition has not sufficed to overturn perceptions of feminism as foreign. As she notes, 'those who want to continue to keep women of our countries in a position of subordination find it convenient to dismiss feminism as a foreign ideology' (Jayawardena, 1986: Preface).

This perception perpetuates an orientalist dismissal of indigenous feminist expressions and delegitimises contemporary gender equality efforts (Badran, 2007: 24). Nonetheless, the interpretation, adaptation, and reinvention of feminism in various religious and cultural contexts reveal its global dynamism—one that is often ignored by its critics.

Jayawardena's (1986) work, as interpreted by Yuval-Davis (2013: 118), offers a potential resolution to the long-standing deadlock between feminists and nationalists by demonstrating that feminism is neither a purely Western construct nor antithetical to national liberation movements. Her analysis illustrates that commitment to national autonomy does not preclude the struggle for gender equality. In line with this, Anthias and Yuval-Davis (1989: 1) argue that the relationship between women and the state is inextricable, though marked by complexity. Women are simultaneously members of collectivities that shape political projects and subjects of state concern, categorised by their social roles (Anthias & Yuval-Davis, 1989: 6). This dual positioning reveals the contradictory lenses through which women are perceived. While the state attempts to define women's roles, complete control remains elusive due to women's engagement across multiple identities and societal levels—including civil society and the economy—which enables agency beyond state-imposed categories (Anthias & Yuval-Davis, 1989: 6).

Women's relationship with nationalism thus exceeds mere participation; they are also transmitters of cultural and ideological traditions, shaping future generations and symbolising the nation itself. Women often become national icons, with the nation metaphorically constructed as a beloved woman (Anthias & Yuval-Davis, 1989: 9; Baron, 2005). Within anti-colonial, nationalist movements, this symbolic and practical role of women becomes particularly pronounced. Nationalism, broadly defined as a movement for autonomy, sovereignty, and universal citizenship (Werbner & Yuval-Davis, 1999: 1), positioned women as active contributors to national liberation. Jayawardena (1986: 3) highlights how movements for women's emancipation unfolded in tandem with nationalist efforts aimed at achieving independence, constructing national identity, and modernising society. Women were central to these struggles, and for many, nationalism appeared to offer emancipatory potential (Werbner & Yuval-Davis, 1999: 1). However, this potential often went unrealised post-independence, as evidenced in Iran following 1906 and Egypt after 1919, where women's exclusion from public and political life persisted (Werbner & Yuval-Davis, 1999: 1).

At the turn of the twentieth century, women and the family became focal points of reform across Egypt and Iran, where social reformers increasingly engaged with issues such as family law and women's clothing—topics now associated with feminist agendas (Abu-Lughod, 1998: 4). In Egypt, Mitchell notes that nationalist reformers' calls to modernise women into ideal wives and mothers were closely tied to broader projects of national development and population training. Yet, much of the scholarship on nationalism in the MENA region critiques its failure to meaningfully include women, overlooking the ways in which nationalist discourse itself constructed ideals of womanhood and modernity (Abu-Lughod, 1998).

Across many postcolonial contexts, the intersection of imperialism and patriarchy did not yield genuine modernity but instead produced a hybrid social formation—what Sharabi terms 'modernised patriarchy' or neopatriarchy (cited in Moghissi, 1999: 84). Mernissi (also cited in Moghissi, 1999: 84) critiques this as a 'mutilated modernity', one that failed to deliver democratic gains for women. The Iranian case similarly illustrates how structural limitations undermined reforms intended to advance gender equality. Rather than dismantling patriarchal systems, the modernising Iranian state reinforced class divides among women and fragmented activist movements (Moghissi, 1999). These cases illustrate how nationalist modernisation projects often co-opted women's roles for symbolic nation-building while failing to deliver substantive equality.

Islamic Feminism or Feminist Islam?[2]

Islamic feminism has emerged as a point of both convergence and contention, defined as a discourse and practice rooted in the Islamic paradigm and informed by interpretations of the Qur'an (Badran, 2007: 23). Crucially, feminism itself is not monolithic, with significant divergences across national, cultural, and ideological contexts. However, a unifying thread across these diverse feminist discourses is a shared commitment to more gender-egalitarian rights and participation, as well as a critical engagement with women's reproductive roles (Moghadam, 2013: 252).

One key area of divergence lies in the acceptance of the term 'feminist'. In countries such as Egypt, the term is often rejected for both

[2] This question arose in Moghissi's (1999: 126) work when she wrote '...if Islam and feminism are compatible, which one has to operate within the framework of the other?'.

ideological and pragmatic reasons, particularly due to its perceived association with colonialism, Western liberalism, and disadvantageous global hierarchies (Al-Ali, 2000; Moghadam, 2013). Conversely, in Iran the term is asserted more defiantly, with some women explicitly incorporating both 'feminist' and 'secular' into their political identities, despite the risks posed by religious authorities.

Nevertheless, Islam—whether political, religious, or Islamist—is regarded by some as inherently detrimental to women's rights (Winter cited in Badran, 2001: 47). Badran (2001), however, warns against conflating political and religious Islam and advocates for the examination of feminist discourses beyond the reductive lenses of Orientalism, multiculturalism, or pluralism. Postmodern feminists have similarly cautioned against generalising feminist theory across cultural and geographic boundaries, though critics of postmodernism warn that overemphasising difference risks descending into relativism and political inertia. As Afary (1997) argues, these two perspectives are not necessarily as diametrically opposed as they are often portrayed.

The Iranian debate on Islamic feminism reveals two dominant and conflicting camps. The first engages with Islamic frameworks to seek reform in favour of women's interests, represented by scholars such as Afsaneh Najmabadi (1991, 2000), Nayereh Tohidi (2003), and Ziba Mir-Hosseini (2006, 2009, 2012)—all of whom have transnational educational backgrounds and, in some cases, ties to the Iranian Left and women's movement (Saliba et al., 2002). Najmabadi argues that gender inequality stems from socio-cultural rather than religious sources, thereby leaving room for reinterpretation and transformation. Mir-Hosseini takes this further by identifying emergent gender discourses among reform-minded theologians and the role of 'ordinary' women in challenging patriarchal family laws (Saliba et al., 2002: 24–25).

In contrast, the second camp—represented by Haideh Moghissi (1999, 2005), Shahrzad Mojab (2001), and Hammed Shahidian (2002)—rejects the notion of Islamic feminism altogether. Moghissi (cited in Cooke 2001: 57) views Islamic feminism as an oxymoron. She critiques Islam as inherently hierarchical and incompatible with the gender equality central to feminist ideology. Further, she argues that Islamic feminism lacks a coherent or identifiable movement, claiming its primary advocates are diasporic academics of Muslim background rather than grassroots actors within Muslim-majority societies (Cooke, 2001).

A contentious point within this debate is the framing of resistance to women's reform in Islamic societies as a cultural reaction to colonialism (Moghissi, 1999). This reasoning, Moghissi argues, is as problematic as attributing female subjugation solely to Qur'anic or *Sharīʿah* precepts. She also critiques the term *Islamic feminism* itself for its lexical vagueness and homogenising implications (Moghissi, 1999). Hafez (2011) echoes this through Kandiyoti's (1996) argument that feminism and religion occupy divergent historical and ideological trajectories, rendering their integration conceptually problematic.

In the Egyptian context, where the family is central to societal organisation, women function as intermediaries between domestic roles and secular political aspirations. This dual positioning often places activist women in a precarious situation—particularly when their religious commitments intersect with their gendered subordination (Hafez, 2011). The early Egyptian women's movement itself was interpreted through a binary lens: feminists such as Huda Shaʿarawi were dismissed as Westernised, while figures like Malak Hifni Nasif were seen as authentically Egyptian—though neither identity was definitively grounded in Egyptian socio-political realities (Hafez, 2011).

In Iran, the 'woman question' has deep roots, dating back to the early twentieth-century constitutional movement where debates about women's roles were particularly salient (Paidar, 1996: 51). From this period onward, feminism in Iran became intertwined with nationalism, with secular critiques of women's subordination often operating without direct opposition to Islam (Paidar, 1996). Prior to the emergence of Shi'i modernism in the 1970s, Iran's feminist movements were largely secular. However, following the 1979 revolution, both secular and religious women expressed dissatisfaction with the direction of gender reforms (Paidar, 1996; Keddie, 2001). A collaborative approach emerged in which liberal, Marxist, and Islamist women each interpreted gender inequality through their own ideological frameworks—liberals advocating secular legal reform, Marxists framing inequality as a class and imperialist issue, and Islamists proposing that a return to true Islamic values would remedy women's oppression (Keddie, 2001).

What ultimately emerges is the contested and multifaceted nature of Islamic feminism, as well as the frequent conflation of feminism with Westernisation and the persistent religion/secularism binary. A key critique of the term *Islamic feminism* is its potential to reduce Islam to a singular mode of identification, flattening the experiences of both men and women into a narrow framework (Moghissi, 1999: 135). Similar issues arise with 'secularism', which is also vulnerable to essentialist readings and lexical confusion. Despite their apparent opposition, Islam and secularism often fall into the same discursive trap of homogenisation, obscuring the diverse and dynamic realities of feminist struggle in Muslim contexts.

Secularism: Theory, Reality, and Fluctuations

Egyptian feminists' strategic deployment of 'secular' illustrates semantic tensions (see Chapter 1). As Badran (2009: 27) notes, fundamentalist women distinguished their Islam-based feminism from Turkish secular feminism, with the *Al-Ittihād Al-Nisā'ī Al-Miṣrī* (الْاِتِّحَاد النِّسَائِي المِصْرِي; Egyptian Feminist Union) journal *al-Misriyya* emphasising the centrality of *Sharī'ah* as a source for women's rights. Secularism thus appeared external, foreign, and un-Islamic. Yet, the nationalist reconfiguration of 'secular' within feminist movements, especially post-1882, recast it as territorial rather than theological—a marker of national unity transcending the Ottoman millet system (Badran, 2009).

The boundary between public and private spheres—once sharply demarcated—has blurred through female activism. Women's public participation challenged patriarchal legal structures, with Werbner and Yuval-Davis (1999: 6; 25) noting how the private sphere dissolved into the public through acts of resistance. The public sphere, no longer spatially bounded, instead became a discursive space open to contestation and redefinition, shaped by gendered struggles for autonomy and against welfare retrenchment (Werbner & Yuval-Davis, 1999: 26; 29). While secularism formally entered the public domain, its seepage into private life unfolded through cultural channels—literature, discourse, observation—rather than formal imposition.

Nasserite Egypt embodied a secular nationalism informed by Arab socialism. Rather than adopting Soviet hostility to religion, this model sought a distinctively Arab path to modernity (Hibberd, 2010: 58–59). Hatem (1994: 661) argues that women's enfranchisement and family-centred reforms served as indicators of a secularising ethos that marginalised public religion while cementing state authority over it. The state's monopoly on religion, through its subordination of the *'ulamā'* (عُلَمَاء; A body of Muslim scholars), recalls the Turkish model (Hibbard, 2010: 63–64).

Sadat, however, reversed these secularising currents. His mobilisation of religious discourse and tolerance of Islamist expression eroded the fragile secular consensus (Hibbard, 2010: 75). Iran, by contrast, persisted with *Reza Šah* reforms through the Pahlavi era, implementing gender equality measures, albeit within a national identity stripped of Islamic referents (Strong, 1997: 133; Adib-Moghaddam, 2013: 283). The Shah's secular nationalism sought geopolitical hybridity—a state 'at the crossroads of East and West'—yet the Islamic resurgence pre- and post-1979 signalled deep discontent.

The Iranian Revolution epitomised this rupture. Rejecting secular authoritarianism, the 1979 upheaval installed a theocratic regime, underscoring how state secularism, if disconnected from popular legitimacy, can falter (Halliday, 2003: 57). The decade that followed witnessed a pan-regional shift: the Iranian Revolution and Afghan jihad catalysed political Islam as a counterhegemonic force (Hibbard, 2010: 82; Juergensmeyer, 1993: 1).

Under Mubarak, Egypt's religious identity became increasingly unstable. While embracing some liberal reforms, Mubarak—like Sadat—adopted a permissive stance towards Islamist discourses, thereby emboldening them (Hibbard, 2010: 110–111). Despite outward liberalism, Egyptian governance remained enmeshed in secular-religious contestation (Hafez, 2011: 56). The 2011 revolution and the subsequent ousting of Morsi merely intensified these tensions, leaving Egypt's identity suspended between competing secular and religious narratives.

Across the MENA region, then, secularism manifests not as a linear progression but as a cyclical negotiation. Turkey's rigid laicism model provided institutional stability but at the cost of religious pluralism (Başkan, 2014: 159). By contrast, Iran's initial separationism lacked the intra-religious competition that plagued Turkey, facilitating smoother state control (Başkan, 2014: 102; 147–148). In both cases, secularism functioned as a sovereignty-preserving mechanism, suppressing public religion through disparate strategies.

While Western observers heralded the postcolonial wave of nationalism as secular in form (Juergensmeyer, 1993: 11), its local inflections were far from uniform. In Egypt, secularisation as citizenship-building, rather than faith-erasure, became the guiding principle (Hibbard, 2010: 7). Yet this project was constantly subject to reversal—from Nasser's assertive nationalism to Sadat's religious recalibration and Mubarak's ambivalence. What emerges, ultimately, is not the triumph of secularism or religion, but their persistent entwinement.

Women, Religion, and Secularism

The near-universality of gender discrimination across historical and cultural contexts is noted by Baderin (2001), who highlights that pre-eleventh-century English men were legally permitted to sell their wives; asserting that women in pre-Islamic Arabia possessed no codified rights—a position that directly contradicts Ahmed's (1992) argument. The absence of normative gender relations across the MENA region is further evidenced by variables such as education, political participation, employment, and legal status (Moghadam, 2013).

Ahistorical generalisations, often prevalent in Western (feminist) discourse, obscure the distinctive trajectories and identities of countries (Najmabadi, 2000) as diverse as Egypt and Iran. Torstrick (2003: 161), drawing upon the works of Al-Ali and Joseph, underscores the importance of these trajectories, reminding readers that concepts such as secularism and democracy—often lauded for enhancing gender equality in Western contexts—are products of particular historical and cultural developments. Moghadam (2013) similarly emphasises these contextual divergences, arguing that legal codes across the MENA region apply differently and reflect 'gender asymmetry' present in (non) Western contexts.

The visibility of Turkey's secular reforms reverberated across the region. In Iran, *Reza Šah* sought to emulate the Turkish model by enacting top-down secularisation that detached religious law from governance, albeit through autocratic measures and with a conspicuous embrace of Western consumerist aesthetics (Sullivan, 1998: 223). His modernisation project included the controversial banning of the veil and the expansion of rural education for women during the 1970s, but it failed to dismantle the entrenched economic and patriarchal structures that maintained male dominance (Friedl, 1991: 195). Khomeini later condemned the Šah reforms, framing the unveiling of Iranian women as symbolic of their transformation into 'Western puppets', and positioning this rhetoric at the core of his Islamic revival (Rahnema & Nomani, 1990: 11).

By contrast, Egypt's fluctuations between religious and secular approaches to governance reveals a more complex relationship between gender and state ideology. Under Anwar Sadat (1970–1981), the state adopted a paternalistic stance towards women's rights, asserting a protective role that, while extending legal benefits, also reinforced traditional gender hierarchies and female dependency (Hatem, 1994: 664). The metaphor of the 'paternal arm of the state' evoked both state benevolence and patriarchal dominance. Under Hosni Mubarak (1981–2011), the rhetoric shifted towards one of gender sameness, yet the objective of preserving state control over women's public participation remained (Hatem, 1994: 664). Thus, while gender policies evolved across regimes, the underlying structures of power continued to circumscribe women's agency within a broader patriarchal framework.

The complexities inherent in gender-related policymaking are intensified by the multiplicity of legal domains and the involvement of diverse institutional actors (Htun & Weldon, 2010: 208). Comparative studies across sixteen states and one territory have attempted to map trajectories of gender equality, revealing uneven progress. Although certain reforms suggest advancement in some national contexts, a 'substantial deficit in women's rights' persists across all surveyed states and within almost every institutional sphere (Nazir, 2005: 31). This persistent shortfall indicates that formal legislative reform alone is insufficient for achieving substantive gender equality, particularly when institutional structures and cultural norms remain resistant to transformation.

To clarify the conceptual terrain, a working definition of 'secular' in early twentieth-century Egypt and Iran may be articulated as the establishment of political authority through secularising initiatives aimed at modernising the state by delineating religious influence from public governance. In this framework, secularisation functions as a process; secularism denotes the ideological principle of institutional separation; secularity refers to the typology or manifestation of such separation; and the secular is the resultant condition where public institutions operate autonomously from religious authority. This taxonomy underscores the nuanced and context-dependent nature of secular transformations, particularly as they intersect with gender norms and legal reform in postcolonial and theocratic states.

Although secularisation in Egypt and Iran proved transitory, this should not be interpreted as evidence of an inherent incompatibility between secularism and the socio-political fabrics of these states. Rather, the instability of secularisation efforts points to inadequacies in the mode and scope of implementation. A closer examination reveals that, unlike Turkey—where secularism was aggressively institutionalised and embedded at the structural level—both Egypt and Iran engaged in more superficial applications that failed to permeate societal foundations. In Egypt, secularising reforms were primarily externally imposed, particularly under British colonial rule, which sought legal and political modernisation without reshaping deeply rooted familial and religious institutions. Similarly, Reza Khan's modernisation project in Iran, while presenting a façade of secular progress to the international community, rarely extended beyond symbolic or top-down transformations.

Despite formal shifts in law and governance, neither state developed a robust, internally driven secular ethos. Instead, secularisation was often instrumentalised—used as a tool for state consolidation or diplomatic credibility—rather than as a deeply integrated political philosophy. Legal reforms touched the surface of social relations, as seen in selective codifications of family law, but did not challenge the embedded role of religion in structuring gender norms and kinship hierarchies.

This historical trajectory also challenges the assumption that secularism and modernity are inherently synonymous or that Islam stands in opposition to modern political development. The failure of secularism in these contexts does not suggest a fundamental incongruity between Islamic values and modern statehood. Rather, it underscores the need for any secular project to engage with indigenous political cultures and institutional realities. For secularism to be sustainable, it must be embedded not merely in law but in the everyday logic of governance and identity formation—aligned with national interests rather than projected as an external performance for global audiences.

Constitutions, Conflicts, and Crises

The early twentieth century unfolded as a crucible of upheaval, as both Egypt and Iran contended with the violent flux of empire, internal dissent, and constitutional reform. Amid shifting global allegiances and imperial contests, the codification of the Iranian Constitution in 1906 and the Egyptian in 1923 did not simply mark institutional beginnings; they revealed the complex entanglements of nationalism, social order, and familial authority under pressure. Constitutions were not static texts but sites for new, and existing contestations, where crises, conflicts, and competing visions of the state collided; articulating new hierarchies and recalibrating individual agency within the tumult of transformation.

In Egypt, the British occupation of 1882 was originally justified as a temporary stabilising measure, and evolved into a protracted assertion of imperial control. Even the 1922 declaration of Egyptian independence operated under the shadow of British military and administrative entrenchment, with complete independence being gained following the British relinquishment of the state in 1952. The rationale for Britain's long stay extended beyond geopolitics; it was also cloaked in a civilisational narrative. Orientalist logics rendered Egypt a linchpin of empire, a threshold between Africa and Asia whose strategic necessity was repeatedly emphasised through their repeated colonisation by key powers, including the Ottoman Empire and France (Said, 1978). This logic

S. Louden-Cooke, *Gender Equality, Matrimony and Secularism in Egypt and Iran: A Comparative Exploration of Early Twentieth-Century Family Law*, Middle East Today,
https://doi.org/10.1007/978-3-032-00846-6_3

helped justify British interventions framed as 'reform' due to hypothetical financial and administrative concerns, particularly if the suppression of the 'Urabi[1] movement was not sufficient (Farid/Goldschmidt, 1992: 1).

Yet beneath the surface of imperial narratives, Egyptian nationalism gathered strength. The 1919 Revolution became more than an anti-colonial uprising; it was a moment in which political identity coalesced around sovereignty and gendered participation. Women emerged not as passive symbols but as active political subjects, their involvement underlining how nationalist resistance both challenged and relied on familial and social norms.

Iran's revolutionary moment surfaced prior to this in 1906, but with distinct contours. Though never formally colonised, Iran bore the imprints of imperial entanglement in its economy, political elite, and social reforms shaped by both Russian and British pressures. Calls for a written constitution, women's rights, and the end of *Qājār* rule came not merely from elites, but from urban intellectuals, clerics, and disaffected publics alike. Yet the Western imagination consistently reduced Iran to a caricature: a stagnant, irrational Oriental society, recalcitrant to progress (Keddie, 1999: 2). Such readings ignored the *Qājār* dynasty's dual legacy as both enforcers of religious conservatism and patrons of cultural and artistic flourishing. Their 129-year rule bore witness to vibrant movements such as the Babis and revolutionaries, whose defiance of state and clerical authority gained recognition among (foreign) observers and unease among domestic elites (Keddie, 1999, 1: 14).

Iranian and Egyptian responses to empire also manifested differently in gendered spaces. In Iran, veiling norms varied sharply between urban and rural contexts. In cities, upper-class women moved through public space heavily veiled, their social participation confined largely to the domestic. However, beyond urban boundaries, nomadic and rural women worked openly alongside men, their labour integral to household economies. Their autonomy—reflected in mobility and economic participation—stood in contrast to dominant Western images of Muslim womanhood, and also the more secluded experiences of upper-class women, with more freedoms be afforded in the private sphere (Keddie,

[1] The Urabi revolution was a sequence of political and military events between 1879 and 1882 led by Colonel Ahmed Urabi who sought to remove British and French forces from Egypt. However, the revolution came to an end following an increased British presence and is perceived as responsible for the continued British occupation of Egypt.

1999b). Egypt, too, exhibited such variation, though urban reformers increasingly framed the family as the crucible of modernity, seeking to recalibrate gender roles within a nationalist imaginary that remained deeply patriarchal. In both states, property and inheritance laws afforded women some measure of control, grounded in Qur'anic principles, but these legal rights did not necessarily translate into unencumbered agency.

Western interpretations of authority within both states were laced with contradiction. British officials in Egypt believed the realisation of hypothetical issues would best serve both British and Egyptian interests, with Lord Cromer's deployment being under the auspices of political representative (Farid/Goldschmidt, 1992: 1). Despite British presence before the establishment of the 1914 protectorate (Sadiqi & Ennaji, 2011: 58), Egypt maintained the hereditary authority of the Ali dynasty[2]—styled as *khidēv* (خديو; khedive) under the 'Ottoman rule of succession'—with governors adopting the title *khidēv*[3] (Farid/Goldschmidt, 1992: 1). Similarly, travellers to *Qājār* Iran were alternately astonished and dismissive; some saw a regime with vast, culturally embedded authority, and others judged it incapable of effective governance (Abrahamian, 1974: 11). These inconsistencies underscore the malleability of perception—how analytical frameworks (cultural versus administrative) filtered the legibility of power, producing either awe or disdain depending on the observer's vantage point.

Thus, the early twentieth century in Egypt and Iran was not simply a story of imposed reforms or resisted empires. It was a complex negotiation between formal constitutionalism and structures of power—family, religion, class—which mediated both resistance and submission. What emerged was not a clean shift from tradition to modernity but a layered transformation, unevenly felt and constantly contested.

Resistance, Constitutions, and Gender

Political resistance in the 'postcolonial Middle East' unfolds as a tangled choreography of power struggles, with national identity formation deeply entwined in claims to sovereignty and 'the struggle for power'

[2] Following the convention of 1840, Egypt was to remain under the rule of Muhammad Ali and his descendants. Signatories included the Ottoman Empire and Great Britain, along with all of the other great powers (Goldschmidt, 1992: 1).

[3] Persian term which roughly translates to 'viceroy' (Farid / Goldschmidt, 1992: 1).

(Tripp, 2013: 252–253). In Iran, the nineteenth and early twentieth centuries witnessed mounting unease towards foreign domination and autocratic rule, even as a Muslim majority exceeding ninety-five per cent fostered a remarkable religious homogeneity, where religious minorities navigated daily life with few impediments, reflecting the 'tolerance of Islamic Iranians' (Cottam, 1979: 75). Yet this unity simultaneously buttressed Shi 'i Muslim elites' social power, whose position was further complicated by the rise of Iranian nationalism. While nationalism's secular character offered a potential softening of sectarian exclusivity (Cottam, 1979: 75), it also challenged the traditional intertwining of religion and power that had defined Iranian society for centuries.

Against this backdrop, women's voices began to surface publicly, articulating concerns across domestic and political spheres that had long been muted. The role of the *'ulamā'* during this period underscored the fraught entanglement of religion and politics. While many clerics endorsed reformist currents advocating a loosening of religious rigidity, the state's fluctuating fortunes under the *Qājār* dynasty—from the *Šah* request for Russian intervention to his eventual deposition in favour of Ahmad Šah —illustrate the turbulence of political authority (Akhavi, 1980: 25). Echoes of earlier social protest reverberated too, with the Tobacco Protest of 1891–92 remembered as a rehearsal for broader constitutional upheavals (Afary, 1996: 17). This history reveals an uneven geography of dissent, where class, gender, and locality intersected to produce divergent experiences of discontent and political mobilisation.

Such stratified dissent was shaped further by the evolving relationship between the clergy and state. The increasing political power of the *'ulamā'* during *Qājār* rule starkly contrasted with their diminished role under the Safavids, yet both entities remained mutually dependent—the *daulat* (دولت; state) and *dīn* (دين; religion) entwined in a fragile symbiosis (Bayat, 1991: 21; Algar cited in Akhavi, 1980: 25). Clerical critiques echoed familiar charges of corruption and tyranny, reflecting a continuity of oppositional discourse that informed the Constitutional Revolution (Akhavi, 1980: 25).

The 1905–1911 Constitutional Revolution epitomises the complex nexus of competing forces in what was broadly termed the Third World, including Western imperial pressures, internal demands for modernisation, struggles for democracy, women's rights, and conflicts with religious authorities (Afary, 1996: 12). Notably, political unrest was not confined to Tehran; cities such as Tabriz and Shiraz also erupted in protest, though the capital remained the epicentre, home to most religious leaders and merchants (Cottam, 1979: 93). Yet regional fissures emerged, with the urban north—boasting a more substantial middle class—embracing constitutionalism enthusiastically, while southern and rural populations remained largely disengaged (Cottam, 1979: 93).

Discontent with royal excess and entrenched privilege underpinned popular opposition. The *Šah* extravagant land sales and inherited pensions stood in stark contrast to reformist calls for austerity and equitable governance, aligning with figures such as Amin od-Dauleh who championed modernisation (Keddie, 1969: 8–9). Nonetheless, political resistance extended beyond critiques of monarchy to challenge the intertwining of religion and state power, reflecting a broader contest over Iran's future direction.

Foucault's (1982: 794) concept of power relations as 'a strategy of struggle' vividly manifests here, as nationalist fervour intensified under the shadow of Western encroachment. The revolutionary slogans echo sovereign claims, galvanised by symbolic victories such as Japan's defeat of Russia in 1905—a beacon of non-Western resistance that inspired Iranian constitutionalists (Browne, 1910: 2). Economic distress compounded political grievances: inflation surged, with sugar prices rising by a third and wheat prices nearly doubling, exacerbated by trade imbalances and tariffs that sparked merchant strikes (Afary, 1996: 51).

> Between spring of 1905 and summer of 1906 three sets of strikes and protests took place, sometimes concurrently, in Tehran, at the Shah 'Abd al-'Azim Shrine outside Tehran, and in Qum. Each strike attracted a broader number of participants; the earlier ideas of a house of justice and a representative form of government were now popularized and radicalized, leading ultimately to the creation of a much broader institution of democracy in the Majlis.
>
> (Afary, 1996: 51)

In December 1905, this simmering discontent erupted when Tehran's governor, Ahmad 'Ala' al-Dawlah, responded to complaints with force rather than reform. His coercive tactics—most notably, a refusal to reduce sugar prices—met with immediate backlash, resulting in the closure of bazaars, which had thus became a stage of resistance.

In Qum, the final set of strikes intensified as the government launched a campaign of arrests and exile against nationalist leaders (Afary, 1996:

51–53), exposing its inability to quell dissent through legitimacy rather than repression. On 9 August 1906, after months of protest and sustained civil action, the secular constitutionalist movement achieved a decisive breakthrough with the establishment of the National Consultative *Majles* (Afary, 1996: 58) (مجلس; religious council/parliament).

In these moments, Iranian national pride emerged alongside a distinctly masculine ethos: 'A Persian is proud of his country and its past greatness, of his religion, of his sons, and of himself' (Colliver-Rice, 1923: 107). The conspicuous absence of women, and Muslims, from this national narrative foregrounds questions about gender roles and religion within the revolutionary project and the implications of secular constitutionalism for women's rights.

Turning westwards to Egypt, the early twentieth century similarly witnessed a multifaceted resistance forged under the twin pressures of colonial occupation and entrenched patriarchy. Between 1900 and 1919, multiple modes of resistance unfolded, from mass demonstrations to literary production, all bearing the imprint of a nation seeking to reclaim its identity and agency. Although Egyptian and Ottoman Syrian intellectuals authored the majority of these discourses, their accounts did not conform to the recognised conventions of autobiography. As a result, their writings often circulated under alternate genre classifications such as travelogues, reformist essays, or political treatises; masking personal narrative within ostensibly impersonal forms (Booth, 2013). Women's autobiographical writing, though submerged and often unrecognised, began to emerge around the turn of the century, creating foundational discourses for feminist activism in the 1920s (Booth, 2013). Marriage narratives also offered a contested space where writers of both sexes critiqued social norms and imagined modern familial arrangements; yet Egyptian modernity was selectively appropriated, nuanced by local traditions and identities rather than the complete adoption of the Western model (Kholoussy, 2010: 6).

Nationalism in Egypt defied 'monolithic' assumptions, particularly as postcolonial critiques disassembled the singular notion of nationalism (Al-Ali, 2000: 40). During the pre-war and protectorate eras, an adapted Ottoman-British hybrid nationalism predominated, a political imagination that was at least nominally more favourable than prolonged British imperial control (Baron, 1991: 283). Yet imperial power sought to negate Egyptian nationality altogether; Lord Cromer's infamous claim that 'there is no such thing as an Egyptian nationality' (Baron, 1993:

244) rationalised policies aimed at anglicising the population and suppressing indigenous claims.

Within this context, resistance became simultaneously a national and religious imperative, a defiant stance against foreign forces attempting to reshape social and political realities (Tripp, 2013: 10). British imperialism cloaked in secular liberalism and capitalism functioned as a hegemonic regime seeking regional domination—a '200-year' trajectory that deeply marked Egypt's historical experience (Tripp, 2013: 178). Yet, as Fanon's (1963) insights on Algeria remind us, this colonial experience was fractured and variegated, resisting simplistic generalisations.

Egypt's World War One reclassification as a British protectorate exposed the thin veil masking direct colonial control. Despite nominal Ottoman ties, British strategic interests overtook Egyptian sovereignty, eroding national identity and sparking a crescendo of nationalist demands (Goldstein, 2002: 67; R.I.I.A., 1952: 4). The 1919 revolution emphasised these frustrations, mobilising diverse social strata, particularly the economically marginalised lower classes, whose hardships fuelled widespread unrest (Tignor, 1976: 44). The press amplified critiques of foreign economic exploitation, further galvanising calls for Egyptian-controlled enterprises reflecting national aspirations (Tignor, 1976: 44).

Within this nationalist ferment, multiple factions coalesced, seeking not only political independence from British and Ottoman overlords but also cultural and economic sovereignty. The symbolic use of tradition and institution as markers of resistance sparked an anti-European sentiment that extended to contestations over gender equality and societal norms (Megahead & Lack, 2013: 205).

Constitutional Revolutions

The early twentieth century in Iran and Egypt was punctuated by revolutionary upheavals often heralded as seminal moments in the emergence of feminist activism intertwined with nationalist struggles. Yet, a closer comparative analysis reveals that women's political engagement in both contexts pre-dates these upheavals and is deeply embedded within complex intersections of patriarchy, class, religion, and colonialism. Rather than discrete starting points, the Iranian Constitutional Revolution (1905–1911) and the Egyptian 1919 Revolution functioned as accelerants in longer trajectories of secular and feminist activism shaped by local and global power dynamics.

In Iran, the Constitutional Revolution generated new, though often covert, spaces for women's political participation. Women's activism encompassed clandestine support for reformist male allies, intellectual engagement in literary salons, and advocacy for educational and legal reforms, marking a critical expansion of women's visibility in public and political life. Consequently, grassroots women's activism and diverse feminist expressions were marginalised, echoing a persistent silencing of female agency within nationalist narratives. This marginalisation mirrors a pattern seen in Egypt, where male reformists like Qasim Amin framed women's issues largely through Western modernisation ideals, sidelining authentic female voices and agency (Baron, 1991). Gayatri Spivak's (2010) concept of the 'subaltern woman's disappearance' in colonial and postcolonial histories resonates here, as such male-centred discourses reinforce reductive binaries of 'tradition' versus 'modernity' that obscure the heterogeneity of women's experiences.

Gender in Iran and Egypt cannot be isolated from intersecting identities of class, religion, ethnicity, and regional belonging, which profoundly shaped women's roles within nationalist-feminist movements.

> Differential positionings in ethnic, racial, class, age, ability, sexual and other social divisions interface with gender divisions, so that although women usually are constructed and treated by various agencies as different to men, "women" as well as "men" do not constitute homogenous categories as either social agents or social objects.
>
> (Yuval-Davis, 1997: 116)

In the early twentieth century, urban elite women were at the forefront of literary salons, political societies, and educational reform circles, while rural and working-class women remained largely excluded from these formal avenues of activism. The influence of conservative Shia clerical authorities further complicated the terrain, as they sought to delimit the boundaries of legitimate feminist-nationalist discourse. These tensions reveal how the interlocking hierarchies of class, religion, and gender shaped the contours of women's participation in the nationalist movement.

During the Constitutional Revolution, the concept of '*Erāde-yi-i Millī*' (اراده ملی; national will) gained prominence across various segments of Iranian society (Tavakoli-Targhi, 1990: 77). Women emerged as visible actors in the call for a constitution and liberation from foreign domination, occasionally appearing unveiled in the public sphere to advocate for both national sovereignty and gender equality. These developments coincided with a growing nationalist discourse that reimagined Iranian identity partly through a 'selective remembrance of things pre-Islamic', facilitating a symbolic dislocation between Islam and Iran (Tavakoli-Targhi, 1990: 77).

As an eyewitness to these transformations, *Qājār* Princess Taj al-Saltaneh was deeply influenced by the revolutionary atmosphere, particularly in relation to women's emancipation. Her engagement with women's rights, expressed through her writings and public advocacy, reflected the broader feminist currents of the time. Taj expressed a desire to connect with Western women's movements in Britain, France, and the United States, seeking to travel to Europe and meet these 'freedom-seeking ladies', and gain recognition of the Iranian movement (Amanat in al-Saltaneh/Vanzan & Neshati, n.d./2003: 68).

Having experienced the constraints of child marriage, Taj viewed female education as fundamental to improving women's roles within the family and broader society (Amanat in al-Saltaneh/Vanzan & Neshati, n.d./2003: 69). Her reformist stance extended to critiques of veiling and patriarchal marriage customs. These perspectives placed her ahead of her time, prefiguring the more widespread feminist activism of the 1910s and 1920s, and contrasting sharply with the depoliticised women's initiatives under *Reza Šah* in the 1930s (Amanat in al-Saltaneh/Vanzan & Neshati, n.d./2003: 71).

Beyond the confines of the royal harem, many Iranian women began to reframe their identities (Bamdad, 1977: 25–26), rejecting imposed notions of passivity.

> The women did much to keep the spirit of liberty alive. Having themselves suffered from a double form of oppression, political and social, they were the more eager to foment the great Nationalist movement for the adoption of constitutional forms of government and the inculcation of the Western political, social, commercial and ethical codes. Equally strange is the fact that this yearning by the people received the support of large numbers of the Islamic priests, a class which stood to lose much of its traditional influence and privilege by the contemplated changes.
>
> (Shuster, 1907 cited in Amanat in al-Sultana/Vanzan & Neshati, n.d./2003: 67)

This symbolism is powerfully articulated in the account of 300 veiled women storming the *Majles*, tearing off their veils, and threatening violence to defend national dignity (Shuster, 1907, cited in Bamdad, 1977: 27). Here, the honour of women and the nation converge, reinforcing the gendered metaphor of statehood and reflecting that female activism was both nationalist and anti-patriarchal.

These dynamics were evident in the rhetoric of both male and female reformers. For instance, Akhundov and Abdol Rahim Talebov framed Iranian secular nationalism in maternal terms, addressing their appeals to those living in the 'motherland' (Bayat, 1991: 98). Likewise, references to the 'independence of the motherland' in women's speeches (Bamdad, 1977: 35) underscored the emotional and symbolic resonance of gendered nationalism. As such, the 1906 revolution created an environment conducive to female political engagement, enabled by the intersection of shifting power structures and the rise of feminist consciousness (Sanasarian, 1982: 20).

Women's involvement in revolutionary societies, such as the Women's Freedom Society, of which Taj and her sisters were members, focused exclusively on issues facing Iranian women (Bamdad, 1977: 30). These meetings, although sometimes mixed-gender, were carefully structured, men were present only to support women in developing their public speaking skills and were not allowed to speak themselves (Bamdad, 1977: 30).

Similarly, Egypt's 1919 revolution foregrounded the unprecedented mass mobilisation of women, symbolised by the iconic 'March of the Veiled Woman', which articulated a collective assertion of nationalist and feminist agency (Fluehr-Lobban, 1980: 238). The formation of the *Al-Ittihād Al-Nisā'ī Al-Miṣrī* in 1923 under Huda Shaarawi's leadership is often seen as a direct outcome of this moment. Yet Huda's feminist activism did not emerge in isolation; her earlier work with *Mabarat Muhammad 'Ali*, a philanthropic organisation founded in 1908 providing education and medical aid to underprivileged women and children, underscores a continuity of feminist social welfare and activism predating nationalist upheaval (Talhami, 1996).[4] The involvement of elite Coptic

[4] Princess 'Ain al-Hayat helped Sha'rawi in the development of this group. Later in 1914, these two women established *Jami* 'et al.*-Ruqīyy al-Adabī li-l-Sayyidāt al-Miṣriyyāt* (جَمْعِيَّةُ الرُّقِيِّ الأَدَبِيِّ لِلسَّيِّدَاتِ المِصْرِيَّاتِ; The Society for Literary Advancement of Egyptian Women) and *Jam 'īyat al-Mar'ah al-Jadīdah* (جَمْعِيَّةُ المَرْأَةِ الجَدِيدَةِ; The Society of the New Woman) which provided women with access to lectures on topics such as art, literature, and music (Talhami, 1996: 12).

Christian women such as the Wasefs, Iskanders, and Hannas during the revolution further complicates simplistic portrayals of Egyptian nationalist feminism, revealing a pluralistic movement that negotiated class, religious identity, and political engagement (Talhami, 1996).

The symbiotic but tension-ridden relationship between feminism and nationalism was evident in both contexts. Iranian women's activism intertwined nationalist sovereignty with demands for reforms in education, marriage, and legal rights, often navigating conservative patriarchal and religious resistance that sought to preserve indigenous social orders alongside anti-colonial struggle. Egyptian feminist organisations framed women's liberation within anti-colonial nationalist rhetoric, linking the emancipation of Egypt from British rule with broader goals of women's education and domestic equality (Baron, 1991). Yet, these alignments required strategic compromises. Egyptian women notably deflected blame for their subjugation away from Egyptian men—male allies in nationalist resistance—towards European women and colonial powers, especially regarding mixed marriages (Hatem, 1989). This nuanced stance reveals the complex political calculus of nationalist feminism, where colonial oppression was 'externalised' due to a reluctance to engage with aspects of family law (Asad, 2003).

In both Iran and Egypt, family and marital relations became sites of feminist contestation and nationalist symbolism. Legal reforms aimed at expanding women's rights in marriage and inheritance confronted entrenched patriarchal structures and religious authorities, demonstrating how feminist demands simultaneously challenged indigenous patriarchal control and colonial domination. The distinction between 'enhanced-authority feminists'—who sought expanded roles for women within private and educational spheres—and 'equal-rights feminists'—who pursued full political and economic equality (Conway cited in Baron, 1991)—illuminates the pragmatism of early twentieth-century activism where Baron (1991) situates women of this era within the first definition. Women thus navigated socio-political constraints by selectively deploying symbolic vocabularies that balanced tradition and modernity (Tripp, 1996).

The emergence of formal feminist organisations such as *Al-Ittihād Al-Nisā'ī Al-Miṣrī* in Egypt and parallel literary societies and reformist circles in Iran encapsulates these complex, multifaceted trajectories. Shaarawi's dual leadership in feminist and philanthropic arenas exemplifies how social welfare, education, and nationalist activism were deeply intertwined. In Iran, despite greater religious and patriarchal constraints, women's mobilisation around education and legal reform highlights persistent feminist aspirations shaped by local contexts and global colonial pressures.

Crucially, feminist activism in Egypt transcended Muslim communities, incorporating prominent Christian women from elite Coptic families, such as the Wasefs, Iskanders, and Hannas (Talhami, 1996), evidencing a socio-religious plurality that enriched nationalist-feminist struggles. In contrast, Iran's religious sectarian divisions and rural-urban disparities framed different parameters for feminist mobilisation.

Ultimately, the 1906 Iranian Constitutional and 1919 Egyptian Revolution represent pivotal junctures that propelled women's activism into new public domains, intensifying the entanglement of nationalist and feminist agendas while exposing enduring fault lines of class, religion, and gender. These moments, however, should be understood as continuities, rather than origins, of feminist activism shaped by indigenous social structures and the global impositions of colonialism.

Iran's Constitutional Eras and Gendered Resistance

When the Iranian Constitution was first implemented, it was swiftly revoked before being reinstated, revealing the *Šah* reluctance to cede control to a document capable of diluting his authority. Its character, arguably foreign to Iranian traditions, left women conspicuously unacknowledged, placed legally alongside the insane and the criminal; denied any rights or recognition (Sanasarian, 1982: 19). The constitution itself appeared as a patchwork, stitching together contradictory strands of Muslim religious law, secular ideals, and Western constitutional principles (Sanasarian, 1982: 19). This confusion stemmed partly from the influence of Western-educated advisors involved in its drafting. The text lacked originality and a distinctly national voice, resembling instead a diluted echo of Western monarchies such as Belgium and the Netherlands, infused with religious undertones rather than progressive reform (Sanasarian, 1982: 19).

The constitution's preamble set a tone that intertwined state authority with religious duty, positioning itself as protector of both the Kingdom and its people, while embedding the execution of laws prescribed by the Prophet at its core (FIS, n.d.; Peaslee, 1950: 200; Wright, 1919: 482; "The Persian Constitution," n.d.: 527). References to God, the Prophet, and Islamic law stood prominently before even the first chapter, signalling that despite the growing secularist momentum among some advocates, religious influence remained deeply entrenched.

Chapter 1 opened by establishing the Assembly as grounded in the Firman, asserting its role as the voice of the Iranian nation involved in political and economic affairs in Article 2 (FIS, n.d.; Peaslee, 1950c: 200). Yet, the language of 'inclusion' bore clear exclusions. The absence of women in this political and economic arena reinforced their confinement to the private sphere, barring them from political participation and legitimising the prohibition of female work beyond domestic confines. Such phrasing codified women's marginalisation, effectively foreclosing avenues for emancipation under the constitution.

A somewhat more egalitarian interpretation surfaced in Wright's (1919: 482) reading, which included 'political and domestic affairs'. But 'domestic' here invoked not women's agency but the patriarchal order, represented in a household structure where men maintained financial responsibility and authority, underscoring women's relegation to an enclosed world.

Religious authority was woven tightly into political obligations. Article 11 demanded members of the Assembly swear an oath (FIS, n.d.; Peaslee, 1950: 201; Wright, 1919: 483; "The Persian Constitution," n.d.: 528); with Article Thirty-Two's references to 'his own case' and the pronoun 'him' in regard to complaints or cases made at the National Assembly underscoring women's exclusion from political processes, fortifying patriarchal political structures. These religious motifs persisted in the Supplementary Fundamental Laws (1907), further entwining faith and governance.

Article One declared *Ja'fari Ithnā 'Ashari* (Twelve Imams) Islam the state religion, to be recognised by the *Šah* (FIS, n.d.; Peaslee, 1950a: 206; Wright, 1919: 490; "The Persian Constitution," n.d.: 534). Yet, Reza Khan's secularisation efforts appeared to challenge this mandate. Article 8 claimed that all individuals were entitled to equal rights under Iranian law (FIS, n.d.; Peaslee, 1950a: 207; Wright, 1919: 490; "The Persian Constitution," n.d.: 535), employing ostensibly gender-neutral language. However, the absence of 'citizen', a term traditionally linked to enfranchised men, betrayed the potential reality, and gender equality remained largely aspirational.

Beyond limiting women, the constitution curtailed the *Šah* powers, though this constraint proved fragile. The middle of 1908 saw constitutional upheaval as the Cossack Brigade defeated the *Majles* in rebellion, abruptly ending the First Constitutional Period (Afary, 1996: 119). The initial *Majles* had achieved little (Cronin, 1997: 9), but the revolutionary period from 1909 to 1911 produced 'effective legislation', propelled by a renewed focus on state-building (Cronin, 1997: 9). The constitution was reinstated in 1909, its new *Majles* filled with (state) reform supporters (Cronin, 1997), elected under an electoral law apparently free from class discrimination. Yet, political power remained skewed: voting was dominated by wealthier, more conservative groups due to poor representation in many regions (Keddie, 1999: 61).

New political parties emerged too. The Democrat Party united social democrats and liberal leftists, advocating secular governance, land reform, progressive taxation, centralisation, and equality for women and minorities (Keddie, 1999: 61). In contrast, the Moderate Party drew conservatives from the old ruling class and *'ulamā'*, perpetuating class-based dominance and exposing persistent constitutional contradictions (Keddie, 1999: 61).

Following the establishment of the constitution, women campaigned for political enfranchisement. In 1911, a parliamentary debate on the matter was triggered by *Majles* delegate Hadji Vekil el Roaya, who questioned why women should be denied voting rights. His inquiry was swiftly shut down by Sheikh Assadollah, who claimed that political engagement was incompatible with Islamic etiquette and beyond women's intellectual capacity (The London Times, 1911 cited in Bayat-Philipp, 1978: 301). The rejection of women's suffrage underscored the enduring influence of religious conservatism and the state's reluctance to cede political space to women, despite their proven nationalist credentials.

The established women's organisations of early twentieth-century Iran, however, pursued divergent political objectives. The National Ladies Society (*Anjoman Mokhadarat Vatan*, founded in 1910), for instance, primarily targeted the eradication of foreign occupation, reflecting a view that imperialism was the root cause of Iran's political instability and, by extension, women's subordinate status (Bamdad, 1977: 35). In contrast, the *Anjuman-i Āzādi-yi Zanān* (انجمن آزادی زنان; The Society for the Freedom of Women) (1907) identified internal constraints—particularly the repressive influence of the clergy—as the primary obstacle to gender equality (Sanasarian, 1982: 35). Despite these ideological differences, both groups engaged with the question of gender inequality, albeit through the lens of distinct adversarial structures: colonial domination versus domestic patriarchy.

Numerous other *anjumans* (انجمن; society/organisation) emerged during this period, including: *Ittihādiyah-yi makhfī-i Nisvān* (اتحادیه مخفی نسوان; The Secret Union of Women) (1907); *Anjuman-i Nisvān* (انجمن نسوان; The Society of Women); *Anjuman-i Mukhaddarāt-i Vatan* (انجمن مخدرات وطن; The Society of Ladies of the Homeland) (1910); *Anjuman-i Khvātīn-i Iran* (انجمن خواتین ایران; The Society of Iran's Women) (1910); *Ittihādiyah-yi Nisvān* (اتحادیه نسوان; The Union of Women) (1911); *Anjuman-i Himmat-i Khvātīn* (انجمن همت خواتین; The Society of Women's Efforts) (1911); and *Hay'at-i Khavātīn-i Markazi* (هیئت خواتین مرکزی; The Council of Women of the Centre) (1911) (Afary, 1996).

Despite their ideological and strategic diversity, these associations shared common ground in their opposition to patriarchal structures—whether embedded in colonial or clerical authority. Education emerged as a central concern, seen not only as a tool for individual empowerment but also as a vehicle for national progress and collective emancipation.

Women's public protests against both foreign domination and gendered subjugation were bolstered by the rise of print journalism as a communicative platform. This rapid growth during the Constitutional Revolution provided an outlet for these grievances, and was considered 'one of the most remarkable features of the Constitutional Movement was the rapid development of journalism', with around 90 newspapers reportedly in circulation by 1907 (Browne, 1910: 127).

This period also saw the emergence of male intellectuals—poets, journalists, and parliamentarians—who publicly advocated for women's rights. Figures such as Dehkhoda, who contributed satirical columns to *Sur-i Israfil* (1907–1908), and poets like Iraj Mirza, alongside *Majles* delegates such as Vakil al-Ru'aya and Taqizadeh, used their platforms to support reformist views. Their efforts were echoed in major publications including *Habl al-Matin* (1907–1909), *Musavat* (1907–1908), and *Iran-i Naw* (1909–1911) (Afary, 1996: 178). Although institutional support from the *Majles* did not result in legislative change, it nevertheless marked a level of engagement more significant than what would be seen during the 1979 revolution (Afary, 1996: 178), consequently emphasising the importance of the early twentieth century for challenging sex-based discrimination.

Women's own engagement with writing and print media also grew during this time, especially within elite circles such as the royal harem, which functioned as a space of relative autonomy and cultural production. Many women in the harem were patrons of female poetry, while male poets and royals also composed verses in praise of these women (Parvis-Brookshaw, 2013: 22–23). Outside the harem, however, women's writing was fraught with challenges:

> Writing, with its potential for public communication... could be considered no less a transgression than unveiling. In both, a woman expresses/exposes herself publicly.
>
> (Milani, 1996: 6, cited in Parvis-Brookshaw, 2013: 19)

As such, some women turned to writing to critique gender roles and advocate reform. Two dominant concerns that surfaced in their work were access to education and the practice of polygamy. Reformers posited that educating women and discouraging multiple marriages would create a 'healthy family environment' conducive to raising patriotic citizens (Bayat-Philipp, 1978: 297). Others argued for abolishing the traditional *mahr*, redirecting those resources towards female education—a symbolic prioritisation of intellect over custom.

Satirists like Dikhuda also addressed gender inequities in social customs, ridiculing the erasure of women's individual identities:

> Everyone knows that, among us, it is a shame to call a woman by her own name... While the woman is childless you call her by saying 'hey!'... Calling a woman by her own name is absolutely improper!
>
> (cited in Afary, 1996: 130)

Despite these entrenched attitudes, the launch of women-led publications marked a breakthrough in public discourse. *Dāneš* (دانش; *Knowledge*), Iran's first women's journal, appeared around 1910. In 1913, *Šokūfeh* (شکوفه; Blossom), the oldest women's newspaper, began by focusing on education before evolving into a more opinionated platform that addressed child marriage, nationalism, and imperialism (Sanasarian, 1982: 32). In 1919, *Zabān-e Zanān* (زبان زنان; *Women's Voice*), published by the Women's Association of Isfahan, explicitly denounced the status of Iranian women and became the first periodical to publicly advocate for the abolition of the veil (Afary, 1996: 187). Notably, it was also the first to be registered under a woman's name—Sediqeh Dowlatabadi—making it a landmark in the gender equality movement (Sanasarian, 1982: 32).

While the Iranian women's movement achieved greater traction in the nationalist sphere than in securing gender equality, the diverse roles women played—and the support they received from progressive men—demonstrate an evolving modernist attitude towards gender relations. The proliferation of women's groups and publications signalled growing challenges to patriarchal structures that had long positioned women as subordinate to men (Stanley & Wise, 1993: 204). Though education remained the primary focus, concerns about child marriage, polygamy, and *mahr* reforms highlight a broadened feminist agenda that began to question foundational aspects of gendered power in both private and public life.

Foreign Partitions and World War 1

Iran's political landscape in the early twentieth century was profoundly shaped by the strategic contest between Britain and Russia, whose imperial ambitions transformed the country into a contested geopolitical chessboard. Iranian actors navigated a terrain where sovereignty was curtailed by foreign powers whose interventions were often disguised as protective oversight. British imperial interests, primarily oriented towards safeguarding India, imposed a contradictory stance towards reform. While a strong Iran could serve as a buffer for India, overt support for Iranian reforms risked angering Russia (Cronin, 1997: 4). This strategic ambivalence reveals colonialism as a selective and fragmenting force, which, as Cohn (2013: 5) and Fanon (1963: 127) argue, privileges certain social factions at the expense of others, ultimately sustaining imperial dominance through internal divisions.

The nationalist movement that emerged in Iran was, therefore, fundamentally shaped by anti-imperial sentiment and cultural identity rather than purely political modernism. Ghani's (1998: 298) argument that genuine modern nationalism only consolidated under Reza Khan's secularising state reforms, highlights the tension between traditional cultural-political structures and emergent secular nationalisms under colonial pressure. The constitutional revolution of 1906, triggered by popular discontent with the monarchy's complicity in foreign exploitation, manifested this tension through the alliance of merchants, religious figures, and secret societies resisting economic colonisation (Keddie, 1969: 3–4). The prevalent view that Iran was being 'sold to foreigners' (Keddie, 1969: 3–4), articulates a profound critique not only of foreign dominance but also of internal elites perceived as collaborators, a recurring theme in colonial contexts.

British support for constitutionalism, while ostensibly progressive, was fundamentally instrumental and conditional. Their reluctance to fully back secular reform, coupled with tacit endorsement of religious institutions, functioned as a colonial tactic to preserve influence and avoid provoking Russia. This calculated partiality reveals how imperial powers manipulate local political landscapes, fostering divisions that maintain dependency and weaken unified nationalist movements (Keddie, 1969: 4). The entanglement of Iran in networks of partial colonisation and the persistent contestation of its sovereignty (Marashi, 2008: 17) created a fraught political terrain in which *'internal'* secularism did not emerge in isolation but rather as a response to layered pressures—both foreign and domestic. By mid-1906, that tension surfaced vividly in Tehran's bazaars, where the state's insistence on lowering sugar prices became a flashpoint. As government demands intensified, anti-government vendors, and some *mullas*, took sanctuary within the Royal Mosque of Tehran (Keddie, 1999: 55). This convergence signalled the deepening of the constitutional movement; one that would carry forward until 1911.

Russia's disdainful perception of the constitutional revolution as British meddling (Browne, 1910: 123) further illustrates the imperialist worldview that discounted the agency and capacity of colonised peoples, framing them as pawns in a broader great-power rivalry. The geopolitical realignments following Japan's defeat of Russia (1904–1905) also introduced a new dimension to Iranian nationalism. Japan's victory served as a potent symbol of non-Western modernity and military prowess, while its constitutional monarchy underscored the potential for governance structures that contrasted sharply with Russia's autocracy (Foran, 1998: 17; Tabari, 1983: 54). The irony that the only major Western power without a constitution was Russia, while the sole Asian power with one was Japan, further intensified Iranian demands for reform. However, the 1907 Anglo-Russian Agreement, signed without Iranian consent, underlined the country's eroded sovereignty. By partitioning Iran into spheres of influence, the agreement reinforced imperialist disregard for Iranian self-determination and revealed the collusion of empires in maintaining regional control, especially with the looming German threat and potential outcome of the revolution (Foran, 1989: 15; Bayat, 1991: 196). Britain's prioritisation of southern oil interests over constitutional guarantees (Hermann, 2013: 444) exposes the hypocrisy of imperial 'protectorates' that undermine the very institutions they claim to support, essentially 'undermining constitutional rule' (Keddie, 1999: 59).

By the outbreak of the First World War, Iran's economy was deeply intertwined with British commercial interests, evidenced by the proliferation of British corporations and burgeoning trade such as silk worm eggs and carpets; with trade rising from approximately 1.7 million pounds in 1875 to 4.5 million in 1914 (Foran, 1989: 11–12). This economic dependency was compounded by Russian dominance in the north, creating a bifurcated and weakened economic structure that stifled national development (TNA, FO 416/112, 1932). Britain's wartime policies, aimed at isolating Iran from German and Ottoman influence, further entrenched imperial control by restricting foreign access and suppressing political plurality (Ghani, 1998: 23); a practice which was utilised in Egypt too. It was within this fraught environment that Reza Khan rose to power, leveraging the Cossack Brigade to impose a modernising, secular state order; an assertion of Iranian autonomy that both challenged and adapted to imperial constraints (Akhavi, 1980: 26–27).

In juxtaposition, Egypt's experience under British imperialism during the same period reveals parallels and divergences shaped by distinct colonial logics and wartime exigencies. The formal severance of Ottoman ties in November 1914 and the immediate prohibition of Ottoman ships in Egyptian ports signal British anxiety over imperial security and a pre-emptive consolidation of control (1919: 436). Unlike Iran's fragmented imperial partition, Egypt was swiftly transformed into a British Protectorate—an explicit assertion of British sovereignty that terminated Ottoman suzerainty and entrenched colonial governance (1919: 436). This rapid imposition reveals Britain's prioritisation of Egypt as a strategic asset, particularly its control over the Suez Canal and its role as a gateway to British India.

Egypt's involuntary entry into the war, as an automatic British ally by virtue of colonial status, underscores the denial of political agency typical of imperial rule (Farid/Goldschmidt, 1992: 173). Yet, political actors like Muhammad Farid[5] sought to exploit wartime instability to push for constitutional reform, employing a carefully deferential rhetoric imbued with religious symbolism to navigate the political constraints of colonial

[5] Muhammad Farid (1868–1919) was an influential political leader of Turkish descent. He was a nationalist leader, lawyer, and writer in Egypt. 'Close to Mustafa Kamil, Farid became one of his main political and financial backers'; following Kamil's death in 1908, Farid became second president of the National Party (Goldschmidt, 2000: 53).

domination (Farid/Goldschmidt, 1992: 173–175). This reliance on Islamic language contrasts markedly with the secular nationalist impulses in Iran, reflecting differing modalities of resistance shaped by local histories and colonial strategies. The explicit distinction between 'British' as rulers and 'English/England' as occupiers further illustrates the geopolitical discourses that framed colonial authority and local perceptions thereof (Farid/Goldschmidt, 1992: 173).

The Egyptian economy's fragility was starkly revealed by its dependence on cotton exports, sustained by European capital, which collapsed under British wartime embargoes against enemy nations (Tignor, 1976: 42). The resultant economic depression not only undermined agricultural production but also destabilised social structures, as rising dowries and unemployment disrupted traditional family and gender relations (Kholoussy, 2010: 26). British-imposed economic restrictions thus contributed directly to social unrest and nationalist agitation, highlighting the intersection of imperial economic policies with domestic socio-cultural dynamics. This pattern echoes in Iran's economic subjugation but is distinguished by the gendered consequences evident in Egypt's social fabric.

Britain's militarisation of Egypt—marked by increasing troop deployments and administrative expansion—exacerbated inflation and social hardship, intensifying nationalist resistance despite wartime suppression (Botman, 1991: 25; Baron, 1991: 285). The erosion of British legitimacy, seen as prioritising imperial war efforts over Egyptian welfare, catalysed a shift in nationalist ideology towards liberal territorial nationalism and the incorporation of women's rights into the liberation discourse (Baron, 1991: 285). This dual struggle for national and gender emancipation exemplifies the multifaceted nature of anti-colonial movements, blending political sovereignty with social reform aspirations.

The trajectories of Iran and Egypt during the First World War reveal the paradoxes of colonialism as imperial powers sought to strengthen their control through division, economic exploitation, and political manipulation, yet these very tactics provoked nationalist awakenings and demands for sovereignty. Both states suffered economic dislocation and political disenfranchisement, but their nationalist movements diverged ideologically—Egypt's infused with religious nationalism and liberal territorialism, Iran's evolving towards secular nationalism under authoritarian modernisation.

The exhaustion of France and Britain following the war, coupled with the mandates system, did not inaugurate a new era of stability but instead perpetuated the 'Eastern Question' under new guises, with nationalist resistance intensifying across the MENA region (Goldstein, 2002: 68). The forced loyalty and conscription demanded by colonial authorities in Egypt, alongside economic dependency and political manipulation in Iran, collectively highlight the sustained fragility of imperial rule and the enduring quest for self-determination. Both cases underscore the need to consider international, economic, and socio-cultural variables in understanding nationalist movements and the profound impacts of imperialism on state and societal structures.

Marriage in Crisis (Egypt): Part One

European influence in early twentieth-century Egypt unsettled more than just the political order; it seeped into the intimate spaces of family life, casting shadows over the traditional structure of marriage. As the economy faltered, fewer marriages were celebrated, and the stability of the family—long regarded as a mirror of state stability—began to falter (Tignor, 1976). The figure of the bachelor emerged with growing prominence, stirring anxieties in cultural and political spheres. These unmarried men embodied fears about the disruption of social norms and were seen as emblematic of what Kholoussy (2010: 6) calls 'experiments in colonial modernity'. Yet, absent from this discourse were the unmarried women, their silence speaking volumes about the gendered dynamics at play, where men held decisive power over matrimonial proceedings; reflecting Yoder and Kahn's (1992: 382–384) 'interpersonal power over'.

Modernity, far from a fixed concept, needs tracing as it evolves (Rabinow, 2008); revealing itself in these tensions over family life and marriage. Kholoussy's (2003, 2010) inquiries trace a 'double factor crisis' driven by economic hardship and cultural upheaval, a crisis refracted through the family and reframing nationalist claims to political independence. Among those most scrutinised was the middle-class bachelor—caught between traditional expectations and the pressures of a transforming society. His reluctance to marry was not simply personal choice but a reflection of broader disillusionment:

> ... it [was] not an exaggeration to claim that the new generation of men prefer bachelorhood to marriage because they do not believe that present-day marriage will fulfil any of their dreams.
>
> (Amin, 1899/2000: 81)

For Amin, marriage was no sanctuary of shared joys and sorrows but a contract sustaining patriarchal control within the home, unless women could pierce the veil of ignorance through education (Amin, 1899/2000). The conspicuous absence of unmarried women from this debate spoke to prevailing patriarchal assumptions that diminished female agency and confined their role to the domestic sphere (Amin, 1899/2000).[6]

Compounding these tensions were visible symbols of foreign influence; Western dress, for example, became a marker of crisis. Ahmad al-Sawi Muhammad lamented in *al-Ahram* the impossible standards imposed on Egyptian men, trapped in a society demanding the outward signs of modernity—fez, suit, tram rides, coffeehouses—while their modest earnings barely sufficed. He observed:

> You are the victims of this society that . . . gives you a paltry salary . . . and forces you at the same time to become an effendi, wear a fez and suit,... ride the tram, read the paper, and sit in a coffeehouse. But if you were, my brother, to wear a galabiya . . . you would find thousands . . . happy to marry you.
>
> (cited in Kholoussy, 2010: 7)

Meanwhile, economic strain tightened its grip through the institution of *mahr*. The 1875 Egyptian Islamic Code of Personal Status sought balance, preventing either party from suffering undue hardship in setting the *mahr*. Yet, as Egypt's economy crumbled, reformers called for the capping of *mahr* amounts, highlighting how inflated demands—exacerbated by rising unemployment and wartime disruptions—barred many men from marriage (Kholoussy, 2010: 33). The familial sphere, traditionally private, thus became a battleground reflecting the impacts of foreign occupation and economic decline, entwining the personal with the political.

[6] The stance taken by Amin shares similarities to Mary Wollstonecraft's (1792/2004) in which a scathing overview of women is presented to the reader. This attitude is understood to indirectly critique the patriarchal system and the restrictions which were placed on women. Through the criticism of women and their lack of rights, both Amin and Wollstonecraft can be understood to have circumvented obvious criticisms of patriarchal society while achieving exactly that. A prominent difference which emerges, however, are critical perceptions that Amin sought to enhance male experiences through improving women's status in specific areas (see for example Abu-Lughod, 1998; Ahmed, 1992).

French and British military presence introduced new dynamics, particularly for Egyptian women. French women settlers unsettled established norms, as colonial narratives deflected responsibility for patriarchal oppression by casting blame onto Egyptian men (Talhami, 1996). The unveiling of some Egyptian women and their fraternisation with French men ignited anxieties, with mixed marriages, some of which were illegal, exemplifying the intersection of religion and colonial law (Talhami, 1996: 2). European women were viewed as rivals, perceived to 'steal' Egypt's educated men, fostering nationalist rhetoric steeped in gendered fears of divided loyalties among offspring (Hatem, 1989: 187). Egyptian women mobilised to deter unions with foreigners, reflecting anxieties over identity and social cohesion.

Tensions extended beyond marriage. European women's campaigns for suffrage were perceived as a challenge to Egyptian women's own standing, casting them as inferior and stirring defensive responses among Egyptian nationalists (Nabawiyya Musa cited in Hatem, 1989: 187). Working-class European women, in particular, were depicted as manipulative, 'convincing' middle-class Egyptian men to marry them, while men justified these choices through beliefs in cultural assimilation (Hatem, 1989: 188).

Economic pressures also heightened private sphere anxieties. Families, struggling to meet household expenses, raised *mahr* demands, pushing marriage beyond the reach of many individuals. The presence of foreign women and rising calls for their political rights intensified nationalist resistance, as the family was recognised not only as a social unit but as a crucible where identity and loyalty were forged (Connell, 1987: 121; Urry, 2011: 104–105). The spectre of foreign spouses and the costs wrought by economic decline combined to produce a complex web of resistance.

Monarchical Transitions

The tumultuous eras of World War One, and the inter-war years, cast long shadows over the monarchical transitions in both Iran and Egypt; transitions that illuminate the complex, often contradictory processes through which secularism was negotiated and imposed within these colonial and semi-colonial contexts. Until 1914, the Egyptian experience under *khidēv* Abbas Hilmi II, the seventh ruler of the Muhammad Ali dynasty (Sonbol, 1998: 1). Widely regarded as a fervent nationalist, Abbas Hilmi II first tested the limits of British authority in 1893, initiating confrontations by attempting to purge his cabinet of pro-British officials without consulting Lord Cromer; an assertion of autonomy that met immediate resistance (Goldschmidt, 2000: 2). By the following year, the tightening grip of imperial oversight rendered overt dissent untenable. In response, Abbas retreated into clandestine opposition, founding *The Society for the Revival of the Nation*, a covert body that would quietly evolve into the ideological and organisational precursor of Mustafa Kamil's National Party (Goldschmidt, 2000: 2). Yet, Abbas' nationalism was not immutable; it softened with Cromer's retirement, signalling perhaps a recognition of the futility of direct confrontation, and the rise of Gorst as British agent—who sought collaboration rather than confrontation—ushered in a period of détente (Sonbol, 1998: 12; Goldschmidt, 2000: 3; Hunter, 2007: 49).

Gorst's modus operandi, a sharp departure from Cromer's domineering style, involved aligning British interests with those of the *khidēv*, thereby undermining nationalist currents from within. While this approach mollified tensions, it compromised Abbas' nationalist credibility and alienated hardline colonialists, who preferred overt control to subtle manipulation. The absence of Gorst's visual and historical prominence in contemporary colonial archives further signals his approach's deviation from the imperial orthodoxy. Additionally, Abbas' memoirs are recognised as illustrating 'the harmful effects of the "open door" policy on Egypt' (Sonbol, 1998: 6). When Lord Kitchener replaced Gorst, Abbas' nationalist fervour rekindled, but by then, the Nationalist Party's influence had already dissipated.

Abbas' memoirs reveal a deeply patriotic figure

> I cannot mention all those who, under my rule, devoted themselves to national rebirth; but those who defended the rights and liberty of women merit a place of honour.
>
> (Sonbol, 1998: 177–178)

Male advocates dominate the broader narrative, with approximately twice as much attention being granted to them, while women's contributions, such as those of Malak Hifni Nasif, are obscured behind pseudonyms or secondary identification through male relatives.[7] The emphasis on

[7] Malak Hifni Nasif was recognised through her pen-name, Bahithat al-Badiya, with the other being identified by her husband: 'Bishara Takla and his alert wife…' (Sonbol, 1998: 178; fn 9).

'defending' rights implies a masculine protectorate over women's agency, reinforcing hegemonic masculinity even within reformist discourse.

This gendered framing mirrors Abbas' characterisation of women's societal participation as the 'feminine element' awakening 'energetic and active' but still largely peripheral to the national body politic (Sonbol, 1998: 197). The distancing language illustrates the persistent marginalisation of women within nationalist projects and reflects a broader ambivalence about modernity's gendered implications; a tension equally palpable in contemporaneous Iranian reform efforts.

The replacement of Abbas with his uncle Hussayn Kemil, following the British-imposed abdication in 1914, starkly illustrates imperial power's manipulation of dynastic legitimacy. Kemil's reluctant acceptance of the sultanate under British duress, with the shadow of a 'British candidate' looming (Hassan, 2000: 80), symbolised the erosion of autonomous rule. Abbas' bitter reflection that this transition 'effectively sanctioned the unlimited extension of a so-called temporary occupation' (Sonbol, 1998: 325) encapsulates the colonial usurpation of sovereignty, reducing Egyptian governance to a façade under British hegemony.

The subsequent reign of Fu'ād, viewed by contemporaries as 'anti-British' but ultimately compliant—evidenced by his transition from Sultan to King—signalled an accommodation with colonial authority, further entrenching British dominance (Goldschmidt, 2000: 59; Sonbol, 1998: 140). The evolving dynamics between the *khidēv* authority and British officials underscore a gradual depletion of agency on both sides, confirming Berque's (1972: 263) assessment that both were 'utterly exhausted'. The *khidēv* vacillating stance—oscillating between nationalist rhetoric and conciliatory gestures—reveals a pattern less indicative of a coherent anti-colonial ideology than of a personalist opposition, one shaped by fluctuating responses to distinct British figures such as Cromer, Gorst, and Kitchener. His initial defiance towards Cromer gave way to a more malleable posture under Gorst's comparatively conciliatory administration, a shift that momentarily unsettled the carefully curated equilibrium of British dominance. Yet this ambiguity was swiftly contained. In response, British authorities recalibrated their influence by leveraging dynastic insecurity and ensuring the ascension of figures whose loyalties aligned more closely with imperial interests. The reassertion of control became most visible in Fu'ād's self-coronation as 'King'—a symbolic alignment with the occupying power that transcended mere titulature. This evolution underscores how monarchy and colonial power interwove to facilitate the implementation of secular reforms, which, far from liberating subjects such as women, often reinforced existing patriarchal and imperial hierarchies.

Meanwhile, the Iranian trajectory under the *Qājār* dynasty similarly reflects the contradictions and constraints of modernisation amid imperial encroachment. Early twentieth-century tensions between the *Qājār* monarchy and the Cossack Brigade mirror the struggles to impose European military models for a standing army (Cronin, 1997: 2). Abbas Mirza's commitment to military reform, involving French and British advisers and overseas education, embodied a determined push towards a modern, standing army capable of defending Iranian sovereignty. Yet, entrenched resistance and structural obstacles hindered these efforts, revealing the limits of reform in a fragmented polity under constant foreign pressure.

The British aspiration in 1919 to formalise control over Iran through a protectorate faced fierce nationalist opposition, catalysing the rise of figures like Reza Khan and Sayyed Zia al-Din Tabataba'i, whose 1921 coup would dismantle *Qājār* authority (Keddie, 1999: 77). This resistance was not merely reactionary but rooted in deep apprehensions about the social costs of modernisation. The imposition of a standing army threatened to increase taxation and reduce social welfare, exacerbating economic hardships for an already beleaguered population (Cronin, 1997: 3).

Iran's predicament was further compounded by the geopolitical rivalries of Russia and Britain, whose conflicting interests undermined efforts to consolidate a strong military and centralised government. Russian efforts to maintain Iranian military weakness illustrate how external imperialist dynamics stymied sovereignty (Cronin, 1997: 3). Against this backdrop, Reza Khan's ascent was not merely a personal triumph but a manifestation of broader desires for a modern state apparatus capable of asserting Iranian autonomy within the constraints imposed by imperial powers.

Yet, the legacy of the *Qājār* military's weaknesses and the fiscal burdens of reform haunted Reza Khan's regime. His modernising ambitions, while foundational in creating a centralised state, were burdened by the economic and structural fragilities inherited from a fractured past (Cronin, 1997: 7, 10).

In juxtaposition, the Iranian and Egyptian experiences reveal the complex interplay of nationalism, colonial power, and secular modernisation. Both monarchies faced colonial-imperial manipulation that curtailed genuine sovereignty, yet the forms of accommodation and resistance diverged. Egypt's nationalist elite wavered between confrontation and collaboration, entwined with a gendered nationalist rhetoric that selectively incorporated modernist ideals. Iran's reformers grappled with military modernisation as a core site of contestation, confronting internal resistance and imperial sabotage alike.

Crucially, the gendered and colonial power dynamics underpinning secularism's implementation in both states complicate narratives of progress. The dominance of male nationalist figures, the sidelining of women's rights, and the entrenchment of imperial control reveal secularism less as emancipatory project and more as a terrain where competing hegemonies—patriarchal, colonial, and nationalist—were negotiated and reinforced.

Matrimonial Equality

Marriage, traditionally understood as a union between two individuals, has long served as the cornerstone of familial and, by extension, societal structure. It is within this domestic framework that future members of society are nurtured and socialised. Yet embedded in these structures are power dynamics that have historically marginalised women. Under long-standing traditions, women were positioned as dependants, with their honour—and eventual marriage—managed by male relatives or designated guardians. Such arrangements foreground a system of power wherein influence flows unequally, reinforcing a patriarchal social order (Yoder & Kahn, 1992: 382–384).

While postcolonial feminism consciously seeks to transcend dichotomous thinking, it cannot entirely sidestep the public/private divide, especially where gendered power is encoded into familial roles and legal structures. The entrenchment of the private as political—echoing radical feminist arguments—becomes evident with the institutionalisation of Personal Status Laws. These laws did not merely regulate domestic life but actively delineated power within the family, assigning authority and submission according to gender.

S. Louden-Cooke, *Gender Equality, Matrimony and Secularism in Egypt and Iran: A Comparative Exploration of Early Twentieth Century-Family Law*, Middle East Today, https://doi.org/10.1007/978-3-032-00846-6_4

The Politicisation of the Private Sphere

In early twentieth-century Iran, constitutional shifts such as the 1906 Iranian Constitution and its 1907 Supplementary Fundamental Laws, alongside Reza Khan's increasingly codified marriage regulations, exemplified the incursion of the political into the private sphere. These legislative shifts extended governance into the intimate lives of citizens, particularly women, whose bodies and rights became sites of political contestation. Ostensibly progressive reforms that granted rights to women simultaneously affirmed the dominance of the patriarchal order that gender equality advocates sought to dismantle.

Changes in Iran 'can be thrown into sharper relief as a contrast is initially drawn with the Arab tribal society', which is frequently confused with the broader status quo across the MENA region (Fischer, 1978: 197). This stereotype is rooted in three (mis)perceptions: a sociological rationale for maintaining order in the absence of state authority, derivations of Sunni jurisprudence, and a customary presumption of a man's entitlement to marry his paternal cousin—a right forfeited only in the face of prior claims from another suitor (Fischer, 1978).

The emergence of women's political salons and home-based activism further politicised the domestic space. In both Egypt and Iran, women converted their private dwellings into forums for political discourse, highlighting the absence of institutional avenues for female agency. This transformation—making the private a public, political space—exposed the state's reluctance to support gender emancipation beyond performative gestures (Botman, 1991: 109).

In Egypt, the legacy of the 1919 nationalist movement gave rise to persistent suspicion of (female) activists. Communications dated 25 and 28 December 1921 reveal that Safiyya and Huda were both viewed through the lens of their husbands' identities (TNA, FO 141/511/5, 1921). In a communication to Cairo City Police, instructions were issued that 'Mme. Zaghloul is to be carefully watched' (FO 141/511/5, 1921); a directive grounded more in apprehension over her public visibility and her husband's anti-colonial reputation than in substantiated concerns. The warning to the press not to publish her appeal[1] (TNA,

[1] This appeal was to the Egyptian public, calling on her Egyptian son's to assist her in ensuring the return of her husband from exile (see for example Baron, 2005).

FO141/511/6, 1922) illustrates how state authorities sought to curtail expressions of dissent, especially when articulated by women.

Similarly, Huda was described as 'one of those who have gone back to the Wafd' (TNA, FO 141/511/5, 1921), a phrase that does more than mark political affiliation—it subtly diminishes her agency by linking her identity to her marital status and political party. The dismissive tone suggests disdain, both for the Wafd Party and for those aligned with it, implicitly positioning them as transgressive.

A letter dated 27 November 1924, regarding the murder of Sir Lee Stack,[2] further illustrates the gendered suspicion faced by women in the political sphere. Elwood, writing to Furness, stated that 'Madame Zaghloul has recovered from her emotion, and is inciting her husband to stir up resistance' (TNA, FO 141/511/6). The implication is that Safiyya, rather than her politically seasoned husband, is construed as the instigator. Her emotional recovery is noted, yet her rational engagement is cast as subversive. While the letter ultimately blames Zaghloul for creating the atmosphere that led to Sir Lee Stack's assassination, it nonetheless portrays Safiyya as a 'continuing problem'—a threat whose influence was not to be underestimated. In this framing, the woman becomes the locus of political agitation, and the man, her instrument.

The language of marriage itself carried the weight of ownership and commerce, as observed by Iranian Sattareh Farman Farmaian (1993: 154), who recalled that a married woman 'belonged not to her own family but entirely to her in-laws'. Such phrasing underscores how women were repositioned within patriarchal structures, not as autonomous individuals, but as assets to be transferred. Princess Taj al-Sultana's reflections further expose the personal toll of such transactions. Recounting her own marriage arrangements, she describes the orchestration of her wedding as a series of decisions made by others: 'they began to celebrate' (n.d./2003: 111), she wrote, marking her exclusion. Her resistance—manifested as emotional and psychological distress—was silenced by paternal authority. Her father's wrath, rather than her own pleas, dictated the outcome (n.d./2003). In this, Taj's story becomes emblematic of the broader struggle: a woman's voice drowned out in a world where paternal decisions overruled female autonomy (Walters, 2011: 18).

[2] Sir Lee Stack was the British Governor-General of the Sudan and Egyptian Army Commander. He was assassinated on 19 November 1924.

Authority over women's marriages was not restricted to family. State officials, too, held sway. In one British diplomatic record, an application for marriage was rejected due to the consular regulation barring officers from solemnising marriages involving polygamous or concubinage-recognising faiths (TNA, FO 416/112, 1932: 44). Here, state authority intervenes not only in religious matters but in personal unions, inserting itself as gatekeeper.

The Iranian Civil Code (1928) expanded this politicisation by codifying legal impediments to marriage, with Section 1050 nullifying any marriage knowingly contracted with a woman already married or still within *al-'Iddah*. Notably, it states 'his contract of marriage shall be void and the woman shall be rendered perpetually unlawful to him' (Naqvi, 1968: 151; Taleghany, 1995: 155), positioning the marriage as the man's possession, and the woman as its subject. This clause underscores the unequal distribution of rights, wherein women are bound to monogamy and waiting periods, while men are exempt.

Laws concerning mixed marriages, too, reveal gender asymmetries. A Muslim woman's marriage to a non-Muslim man was strictly prohibited (Section 1059 in Naqvi, 1968: 152; Taleghany, 1995: 156), while silence on the inverse pairing—Muslim men with non-Muslim women—suggests tacit acceptance. Nationality laws compounded this imbalance, with Iranian women who married foreigners having to relinquish their nationality, reclaiming it only through state petition following divorce or widowhood (TNA, FO 416/112, 1932: 44–45). The process not only stripped women of legal identity but demonstrated the extent to which their public and private existence was filtered through male association.

Further restrictions were imposed under Section 1060, requiring state permission for Iranian women marrying foreigners (Naqvi, 1968: 152; Taleghany, 1995: 156). Although similar conditions existed for government officials wishing to marry foreign women, these were applied at discretion, not as obligation. Such inconsistencies underscore the gendered nature of state control.

Legal provisions pertaining to marital conduct also laid bare the state's deep intrusion into the intimate sphere. The Civil Code established that conjugal rights and obligations commenced with the marriage contract (Section 1102 in Naqvi, 1968: 156; Taleghany, 1995: 161), enshrining a 'sexual contract' (Pateman, 1988) under the law. While framed as mutual duty, these stipulations disproportionately regulated female behaviour, casting women in roles of service and submission

(Stanley & Wise, 1993: 75). Sections 1105 and 1117 (in Naqvi, 1968: 156–157; Taleghany, 1995: 161–162), for example, granted husbands the authority to restrict their wives' employment if it was deemed damaging to family honour.

Severe consequences were imposed in instances where legal boundaries were transgressed. Marriages conducted in contravention of legal provisions that resulted in physical harm or death of the woman rendered the husband liable to imprisonment with hard labour (Naqvi, 1968: 158). Thus, the state's legal apparatus did not merely govern the institution of marriage—it transformed it into a political instrument. The personal was rendered political, not only through ideological assertion but through tangible legislation that regulated sexuality, identity, nationality, and domestic life. In rendering the private sphere a site of legal governance, the state drew women into political life—but only as subjects of control.

Choosing a Partner

The marital contract, far from being a neutral legal arrangement, functions as a key instrument in the consolidation of patriarchal control, with women's social positions often being determined and reproduced through the mechanisms of marriage (Mohanty, 2003). This observation becomes material in the structural processes that govern marital arrangements. Engagements are typically orchestrated not by the individuals concerned but by their male relatives—often without the woman having met her future husband beforehand.

In Iran, the legal language surrounding *khāstgārī/khāstgār* ((خواستگاری(خواستگار; A suit/suitor) and engagement codifies this gendered asymmetry. Iranian Civil Code section 1034 permits men to initiate courtship with any eligible woman (Naqvi, 1968a: 148; Taleghany, 1995: 151), but the reciprocal right of women is conspicuously absent. The statute's silence is not neutral—it articulates and enforces a legal imagination in which men act and women are acted upon. The subjectivity of women is not only marginalised; it is structurally effaced.

The engagement itself is framed as 'an unbinding promise of marriage between a man and a woman, whom he can lawfully marry; it is a precursor to marry' (NWRO, n.d.: 22). The formulation is revealing: the promise is legally non-binding and the active subject remains male. Even where rights to compensation exist in cases of unjustified withdrawal, they are circumscribed by time limits and evidentiary burdens (Sections 1035, 1036 and 1039 in Naqvi, 1968a: 148; Taleghany, 1995: 151), reinforcing the fragility of women's position within the contract.

The necessity of paternal or guardian consent deepens this gendered imbalance, reducing the woman to an object of exchange whose eligibility is defined by her legal availability. Under a polygamous system, men may lawfully marry multiple wives, while women's eligibility is restricted not only by existing marriages but by *al-'Iddah* following divorce, or death. The asymmetry is not simply doctrinal, and it is enacted in everyday practices.

Memoirs and biographical accounts offer powerful windows into how legal structures are internalised, resisted, and reproduced. Huda (1987: 11) describes Egyptian betrothals and how 'they were often acquired at a young age'. The choice of word is not incidental—it places women, but predominantly girls, in the realm of property, a theme she later amplifies when referring to her father's land acquisitions (Shaarawi, 1987: 15). The metaphor does not merely describe common female experiences with betrothal; it performs the logic of commodification that marriage arrangements often entail.

Colliver-Rice's (1923: 91) account underscores similarities in Iran and the structural silencing of women where 'She is betrothed and married as a child without the slightest reference to her own wishes or ideas, in fact without any knowledge, on her part, of the man to whom she is to be married'. The use of the passive voice—'betrothed and married'—denotes an absence of agency that is not accidental, but fundamental. This passivity is further rationalised through appeals to female youth and seclusion. This architecture of dependence is illustrated by Sattareh, who despite having a father who advocated for women's education, retained strong beliefs in establishing domestic skills so to enhance her suitability as a wife:

> Naturally, I had no way of looking for a husband myself. Western-style courtship was unknown; a girl sat in the andarun and waited until her father or brother or cousin found her someone, and if they couldn't, she was out of luck and had to spend the rest of her life being looked after by her brothers or other male relatives.
>
> (Farman Farmaian, 1993: 114)

The ellipses, the finality of 'out of luck', and the imagery of passive waiting frame a social reality where women's futures hinge on the actions—or inactions—of male relatives. The language does not merely describe her circumstances; it captures the sense of foreclosed possibility, with an unmarried women being burdensome on her male relatives.

Huda's reaction to learning of her betrothal further reveals the affective dimensions of this system. Overhearing her mother and 'Aunt' Gazibiyya Hanim, who were responsible for her marriage following the passing of her father, discussing the matter, she recalls that 'the room began to spin' upon hearing them say 'If necessary...we could arrange a marriage with her cousin' (Shaarawi, 1987: 52). The physiological response—dizziness, disorientation—suggests a visceral recognition of dispossession. Similarly, Taj is not consulted about her marriage. Her father simply informs her: 'I will have you married soon. I will come to your home often and you must serve me' (al-Sultana/Vanzan & Neshati, n.d./2003: 144). The language is authoritative, devoid of ambiguity, with 'serve' rendering the conjugal relationship not as a partnership but as a hierarchy, replicating the domestic power structures from which she was being displaced. Her preparation 'to love him' reads not as a declaration of emotional openness but as a pre-emptive submission to the inevitability of her circumstances. This conversation was, however, preceded by an altercation with her mother, with this socially accepted custom offering her a potential escape when she was older.

The wedding ceremony itself underscores the violence of coerced conformity. Taj recounts how:

> The vow was said and everyone waited for my response. But tears left me no reprieve for a reply, and I was trembling all over. Finally, after painstaking efforts, and several clandestine beatings, I said a feeble aye," thereby winning release from the turmoil and confusion of the moment... Oh, what a cursed day, what an evil hour! Never will I forget that moment. When freedom and dignity were snatched away from me and replaced with antipathy and revulsion. Holding that damnable day as the author of my ruin, I will denounce it forever.
>
> (al-Sultana/Vanzan & Neshati, n.d./2003: 111–112)

Her recollection layers emotional coercion atop physical violence, exposing the hollowness of 'consent' secured through intimidation and social expectations. The marriage ceremony, meant to be a moment of union, becomes instead an enactment of subjugation. Even within her critiques of customs and traditions which she developed from a young age, Taj reproduces prevailing gender logics.

> Ah misery! Of mankind's great misfortunes one is this, that one must take a wife or husband according to the wishes of one's parents...Man must always choose his eternal companion well, and get to know her thoroughly before making his choice, so that he does not ruin his life and fall prey to temptation.
>
> (al-Sultana/Vanzan & Neshati, n.d./2003: 108)

Despite her evident disapproval, the linguistic centring of male agency—*his* choice—illustrates how deeply entrenched patriarchal norms are, even in dissent. Moreover, she believed that unhappiness due to ignorance about their future spouse and being unable to make an educated decision would potentially result in extra marital indiscretions.

Doria Shafik's intervention provides an important point of contrast. At age 12, upon her mother's death, she asked to have her engagement annulled (Nelson, 1996: 22). The act of 'asking' may appear deferential, but it signals a rupture in the expected script and signifies respect towards her grandmother while acknowledging the significance of her request. Her description of her betrothal to al-Sa'id al-Qasabi as 'this' suggests a refusal to be emotionally implicated in a decision she did not make. Her defiance, though understated, indicates an emergent feminist consciousness, an understanding of self-determination and achieving personal satisfaction without a predetermined future; characteristics shared with Huda, and in part Sattareh, but not with Taj. This could in part have been shaped by class mobility and educational access, with age and expectation also being prominent factors.

Legal reforms proposed in Egypt during the 1920s attempted to formalise some degree of female contractual agency. The 1926 committee recommendation allowing wives to include stipulations in marriage contracts was approved by the Cabinet but vetoed by King Fu'ād in response to public backlash (Shaham, 1999: 465, 475), later omitting it form the 1929 law. That the proposal even reached Cabinet reflects the growing pressure for reform, but the veto—justified by appeals to the *Ḥanafī* orthodoxy—demonstrates the entrenched resistance to any expansion of female agency. Due to the rigid nature of the *Ḥanafī* doctrine, and Egyptian legislators having adopted *takhayyur* (principle of selection) in

1920, a compromise was to adopt the *Ḥanbalī* position, which allowed stipulations providing they adhered to *Sharīʿa* (Shaham, 1999: 476). Despite the initial vetoing of this proposal, stipulations had been an informal tradition prior to 1926; yet even where contractual clauses were used—as in Huda's case—the negotiation was typically carried out by parents, not the brides themselves (Shaarawi, 1987: 24).

In Iran, such stipulations invalidated a marriage, with a marriage contract including a revocatory condition could be ruled invalid. Under Sections 1068–1069 of the Civil Code (Naqvi, 1968: 152; Taleghany, 1995: 157), even the *mahr* could be retroactively annulled if framed within time-bound conditions. The contractual space left to women was thus rendered legally precarious, with the metaphorical framing of the marriage process frequently revealing its transactional core. Sattareh (1993: 155) likens it to fishing: 'If a man swam into Shazdeh's net whom he and Khanom considered suitable, I would have no choice but to obey'. The imagery of a net, of capture, inverts the logic of romantic choice into one of entrapment. Sattareh's (1993: 157) father's evaluation of a *khāstgār* via an 'interview' similarly reduces courtship to a method akin to professional vetting.

Marriage, in this context, becomes a terrain where patriarchal authority is not only exercised but reproduced through legal and familial structures. As Kaufman (1994: 63) argues, the passage into normative masculinity is mediated by such institutional practices, with marriage serving as both a rite of passage and a mechanism of control. The stories presented here are not simply accounts of individual suffering within the patriarchal structures surrounding the establishment and extension of the family, but they are structural critiques embedded in lived experience.

Wali and Mahr

The role of the *wali* (marriage guardian) across Islamic legal schools exhibits significant variation, yet a commonality persists in the authority granted to 'marriage guardians' to contract marriages on behalf of children of both sexes without their consent (Coulson & Hinchcliffe, 1978: 39). This legal prerogative is emblematic of broader gendered dynamics, where female agency in marital arrangements is routinely curtailed. Within Hanafi jurisprudence, a crucial nuance emerges: a marriage contracted by a guardian other than the paternal father or grandfather may be annulled by the individual upon reaching puberty. In contrast, for women adhering to other Islamic traditions, consent remained elusive—even in adulthood—until after their initial marriage had already been concluded, often without their volition (Coulson & Hinchcliffe, 1978: 39). Such legal distinctions dislodge assumptions of a monolithic Islamic legal framework and instead foreground its interpretive pluralism.

Iran's Civil Code further codified patriarchal control. Section 1071 permitted either party to delegate a third person to conclude the marriage contract (Naqvi, 1968: 153), yet this formal permission did not signify autonomy for women. Until the age of eighteen, a woman could not legally marry without her guardian's approval (Section 1042 in Naqvi, 1968: 149). This approval, as per Section 1043 (Naqvi, 1968: 149), had to come specifically from the father or paternal grandfather, thereby entrenching patriarchal lineage as a legal necessity. Even upon reaching adulthood, a woman remained subject to male oversight unless procedural obstacles—such as refusal by the guardian without just cause—necessitated institutional intervention. In such cases, a woman could petition the Marriage Registration Office, which, after notifying the guardian and awaiting a fifteen-day response period, could solemnise the union (Naqvi, 1968: 149). This process subtly exposes the underlying structure: legal mechanisms were in place not to secure female consent per se, but to mediate patriarchal failures.

The legal specification that only paternal figures held valid authority, and not alternative male guardians in their absence, reveals a tightly controlled patriarchal transmission of power. Women's dependence upon male family members was thus structurally enforced, not circumstantial, and this is echoed in the personal histories of women such as Sattareh and Taj, where fathers orchestrated their betrothals. However, Anis al-Dawla, head of the harem, took on this responsibility for Taj in her father's absence, again signalling a transfer of authority rather than empowerment (Amanat in al-Sultana/Vanzan & Neshati, n.d./2003: 34). Similarly, following the death of Huda's father, her cousin became her *wali*, only to later become her betrothed. The convergence of guardianship and matrimonial interest raises critical ethical questions, especially when Huda was asked, 'Whom do you wish to designate as your wakil to sign the marriage contract?' (Shaarawi, 1987: 54). Although she was nominally offered a choice of who would become her *wali*, the key decision—whom to marry—had already been made on her behalf, reflecting the performative nature of consent in such contexts.

The entrenchment of male control over marital arrangements drew feminist critique in Egypt and Iran, where women increasingly questioned the legitimacy of their marginalisation in such pivotal decisions. Kholoussy (2010: 115) highlights the Egyptian feminist discourse as one that directly questioned 'the Egyptian father's authority'. The *wali* thus functioned not simply as a legal figure but as a custodian of familial ownership—reinforcing a patriarchal, transactional model of marriage where women were effectively treated as property.

This commodification was further entrenched through the practice of *mahr*, the bridal gift. While theoretically a financial security for the bride, *mahr* often reinforced transactional perceptions of marriage. Coulson and Hinchcliffe (1978: 200) observe that while the bride could demand it at will, it was commonly paid in two parts with an small 'advance' signifying a woman's acceptance, with the remainder being paid upon divorce, reinforcing male financial control, but also serving as a disincentive for him to divorce her. Moreover, its social value often mirrored the status of the bride's family, effectively codifying class hierarchies through the institution of marriage. The advance payment—sometimes referred to as the 'šir baha' (شیر بها; milk price) purportedly compensated the mother for raising the daughter, yet simultaneously echoed deeper anxieties around the perceived burden of female offspring.

Critics such as Kasravi (cited in Regan, 1985: 70) challenged the necessity of *mahr*, reframing marriage as a mutual union rather than a commercial exchange. This critique underscores the economic precarity facing families with multiple daughters, for whom *mahr* obligations became burdensome rather than protective. Hence, *mahr* became not only a reflection of male honour and wealth but also a negotiation of familial liability. Moreover, justifications reflected protecting women from destitution should she be divorced, while also serving as a potential source of profit for fathers.

In early twentieth-century Egypt, instalment-based payments were common, with advances often representing one-third to one-half of the total (Kholoussy, 2010: 28). These financial arrangements—reserved and deferred—mirrored the economic logic of transactional contracts, further reducing women to commodities. Huda's recollection of choosing jewellery to mark her betrothal reveals the seductive allure of material goods in obscuring her lack of agency. The gifts were not symbols of affection, but tokens of transactional fulfilment: 'I found a casket of jewels lying open in front of her; she asked me to select some pieces in fulfilment of a vow she had made for the recovery of my illness' (Shaarawi, 1987: 52). Her innocent excitement merely underscores the extent to which consent was aestheticised, not actualised. Youth was also a determining factor, with Huda having been married at 13, as it was believed that there would be more compliance from the bride.

Taj's experience was starker still. In a carefully orchestrated scene, trays of toys and jewellery were presented before her in the presence of a boy who, after initially choosing her elder sister, was redirected by Taj's father:

> As soon as my father had spoken, the boy picked up a ring and put it on my Sisters finger, saying, "S-s-s-sir, I ch-ch-ch-choose th-th-this girl as my b-b-b-betrothed!" My father embraced him and said, "My dear Aziz! Your betrothed is this Other girl, and it is my wish that you have her.
>
> (al-Sultana/Vanzan & Neshati, 2003: 100)

Here, the illusion of choice was once again shattered and parental authority overrode personal preference, and obedience was instilled through spectacle and ritual for children of both sexes.

Iranian law further systematised *mahr*, detailing permissible forms and conditions for its transfer (Sections 1078–1101 in Naqvi, 1968: 153–156). The contractual emphasis was not on relational equality, but on securing rights in the event of marital breakdown. If *mahr* was unpaid, consummation of the marriage could be legally withheld without forfeiting maintenance (Naqvi, 1968: 154). However, once consummated, the woman's leverage diminished significantly. These stipulations institutionalised the risk management logic underlying marriage, where women's rights were contingent upon compliance and meeting expectations.

In cases of divorce, the portion of *mahr* awarded depended on whether the marriage had been consummated and whether an amount had been agreed. If unspecified, the woman was entitled to a standard amount *mahr al-Mut'ah* (مَهْرُ الْمُتْعَةِ; dower for specific divorce/*sigheh*), and is divorced subsequently she was entitled to *mahr al-Mithl* (مَهْرُ الْمِثْلِ; equivalent dower), yet even this was calculated in light of the husband's financial status (Sections 1092–1094 in Naqvi, 1968: 155). *Sigheh* added further complications, with *mahr* being non-negotiable for legal validity (Sections 1095–1097 in Naqvi, 1968: 155). Upon a woman's death, her *mahr* remained intact, and if the marriage proved void, and the woman had been unaware, consummation preserved her right to *mahr*; if not mentioned, the marriage was annulled (Section 1099, Naqvi, 1968: 155).

The materialism underpinning these arrangements was not lost on feminists like Doria Shafik. Her marriage to her cousin, Nour, with whom she was reunited in 1937 while undertaking two theses at the Sorbonne, was conducted without parental consent and without accepting *mahr*, which was a radical act that rejected commodification in favour of mutual equality (Nelson, 1996: 92). By disavowing *mahr*, Doria symbolically disrupted the transactional nature of traditional marriage and reasserted a model rooted in autonomy and reciprocity.

Marriage in Crisis: Part 2

Despite Colliver-Rice's (1923: 107) observation that 'Bachelors are not found in Moslem lands', one of Iran's major social concerns was that 'men are not marrying' due to difficulties in finding 'honourable women' (Kasravi, cited in Regan, 1985: 69). This state of bachelorhood, however, transcended a mere demographic phenomenon. It served as a symbolic position—particularly in Egypt and, to a degree, Iran—against the backdrop of colonial intrusion. The national body became personified through bachelorhood: Egypt was cast as an unmarried man projecting its desired postcolonial autonomy (Kholoussy, 2010: 11).

Such gendered national metaphors were not anomalous. Baron (2005: 11, 7) notes the prevalence of familial symbolism within Egypt's nationalist movements: Safiyya Zaghlul as 'Mother of the Egyptians' and the feminisation of the nation through *Miṣr* (مِصْرُ; Egypt), a grammatically feminine noun. Yet, this femininity was complicated. Baron (2005: 7) acknowledges that while *Miṣr* is female, *waṭan* (وَطَنٌ; homeland) assumes a masculine gender, revealing a dual-gendered construction of the Egyptian state. These metaphors found tangible expression in the everyday decisions of citizens, where personal choices—such as remaining unmarried—mirrored nationalist values, revealing the permeability between public ideology (increasingly secular) and private life (usually more religiously influenced).

Such metaphorical dimensions did not remain unchallenged. Mustafa Sadiq al-Rafi'i (cited in Kholoussy, 2010: 23) described marriage as both the fulfilment of manhood and an act of national allegiance: 'Marriage is the cornerstone of manhood and a principle of national allegiance. A man who does not marry is like a deserter from the army: Both betray their responsibility and duty to their nation. Manhood can only be attained through marriage'. Here, marriage was imbued with political weight, and bachelorhood reimagined as betrayal. The marital crisis of 1934 thus became a site where anxieties over masculinity and nationalism converged, with men's choices scrutinised through a nationalist lens.

This scrutiny extended beyond Egypt's borders. Iranian bachelorhood echoed similar concerns, with nationalist and constitutionalist discourses aligning personal freedom with national sovereignty. Secular reform and political autonomy were tethered to transformations in political practices, with one notable parallel being the economic challenge surrounding *mahr*. In Egypt, economic instability inflated *mahr* to unattainable levels for many suitors; in Iran, the issue lay in the inability of fathers to provide one (Regan, 1985: 71). Consequently, girls remained unmarried, and their honour questioned due to the 'unfortunate situations' surrounding them (Regan, 1985: 69). These dynamics reveal the intersection of state dynamics, economic stability, class, gender, and morality within the broader considerations of marriage.

Egypt's marriage crisis also catalysed a reimagining of the state's role. The public discourse evolved, blaming arranged marriages in 1920, and by 1931, the public/private dichotomy became the target (Kholoussy, 2010: 52). These narratives resonated with the critiques of early reformers such as Amin (1899, 1900/2000), as well as Taj (n.d./2003) and Sattareh (1993). When these critiques waned, public scorn turned towards 'debauched women' (Kholoussy, 2010: 55), underscoring that no singular cause could explain the decline in marriage rates in both states. This fragmentation illustrates the multidimensional nature of social crises and highlights how moral panics are constructed and gendered.

One particularly fraught issue was the early age of marriage. Girls, sometimes as young as twelve, were married to significantly older men—a practice that not only jeopardised their physical and psychological development but also intensified the power imbalance between spouses. This links to a broader crisis of stolen childhood, health concerns, and coerced submission, thus moving beyond Kholoussy's (2003, 2010) initial definition.

Egypt's Law 56/1923 was perceived as 'much more pro-feminist' (Talhami, 1996: 106–107) as it addressed these concerns by invalidating marriages where the girl or boy was under sixteen or eighteen respectively, if challenged in court (Talhami, 1996: 107). However, the law stopped short of criminalising such unions, highlighting the gap between legislative intent and enforcement. Patriarchal justifications remained strong: Harik and Marston (1996) note that traditional fathers often sought early marriages for daughters to relieve financial burdens and preserve family honour. Moreover, the perceived malleability of young brides ensured their easier integration into the husband's familial structure, reinforcing patriarchal hierarchies through the mechanism of *ṭāʿah* (طاعةٌ; obedience)[3] which reduces the risk of tension among women (Gillis et al., 2007). In marrying young, a girl was expected to internalise submission, effectively transitioning from paternal to spousal authority without interruption and thus reducing the likelihood of *nāshiz* (نَاشِزٌ; disobedience).

Huda's life exemplifies the personal cost of such practices. Married to her cousin (and guardian) at thirteen (Fay, 2003: 94), she later channelled her experiences into activism. In the 1920s, the *Al-Ittiḥād Al-Nisāʾī Al-Miṣrī* petitioned the government to establish a minimum marriage age, leading to legislation that set these at sixteen for girls and eighteen for boys (Sadiqi & Ennaji, 2011: 136). This advocacy extended beyond law; it was a call to protect education, health, and childhood, while indicating a shift away from religious paradigms where numerical benchmarks were not confirmed. In Iran, personal recollections also illustrate the emotional toll of early marriage. Taj (n.d./2003: 167–168) recalled her child marriage and its deteriorating consequences, noting the emotional immaturity of both partners and the trauma of being married at eight. Her narrative critiques not just the age, but the absence of consent and agency, which rendered her a stranger in her own life.

The marginalisation of women who defied or were victims of these norms is clearly illustrated in Colliver-Rice's (1923: 146–147) account of a young orphan girl in a village near Isfahan.

> ...they told me that her father had left her some money,...It was soon known in the village that she had money, and she was married when very young to a man thirty years her senior. He represented to her guardians that he wanted to start business as a muleteer, and persuaded them to

[3] Obedience, or *ṭāʿah* is regarded to be a legal obligation since *Shari'a* is understood to have made marital rights and duties 'mutual and complementary' (NWRO, n.d.: 30).

> let him have his wife's money to buy mules and pack-saddles. Very soon after this he and his mules set out on a journey and were never seen nor heard of again. The child's money had all gone, and she was dependent on her aunt, and her future seemed very uncertain...She went to school, and proved clever and promising, and thoroughly enjoyed the freedom of her new life...the mother of another pupil came to see me, and said: "I am not going to send my daughter to the school any more, and some of the other mothers say they will take their girls away too." I asked the reason for this, and she said: "We don't think it good that a girl who has been married should come to school with our girls. Her mind has been poisoned with all that she has seen and known, and she is not fit to mix with our daughters."...

Here, social ostracism compounded the material vulnerabilities already inflicted by marriage.

Iran's legal reforms addressed such issues unevenly. Section 3 of the Iranian Marriage Act imposed prison sentences for marrying underage girls—as was stipulated in Section 1041 of the Civil Code—with stricter penalties if the bride was under thirteen (Naqvi, 1968: 158). Yet Sattareh (1993: 50) recounted cases where girls were married as young as nine due to the benchmark being puberty, thereby indicating that traditional customs, as in Egypt, continued to supersede legal standards.

Even where legal frameworks existed, enforcement remained patchy. In Egypt, document falsification enabled the circumvention of marriage age laws (Sadiqi & Ennaji, 2011: 136). Nonetheless, the legislation represented progress across three fronts: it postponed marriage in favour of education, addressed women's health by mitigating the risks of early childbirth, and responded to feminist concerns about bodily autonomy.

Iranian feminist media, such as *Patriotic Women*, echoed these concerns, warning against the dangers of child marriage (Sanasarian, 1982: 36). Despite emerging from elite backgrounds, many Iranian feminists had themselves endured degrading marital conditions—suggesting that these issues transcended class (Sanasarian, 1982: 46). Despite seeking more secular approaches, both Iranian and Egyptian feminists avoided criticising Islam directly. Instead, they condemned patriarchal interpretations that justified female seclusion (Sanasarian, 1982: 47), asserting that women's rights were not antithetical to Islam but rather stifled by its politicised, male-centric readings. Moreover, increasingly secular legal and political vocabulary indicated changes while retaining religious and patriarchal customs.

Marriage also became a site of public health discourse. Section C2 of the Iranian Marriage Act mandated medical certification prior to marriage, though girls were exempt from presenting documentation regarding venereal diseases (Naqvi, 1968: 161). This exemption hinged on the presumption of virginity, itself a deeply gendered and potentially age related assumption. Moreover, Section 5 of the law penalised deception in marriage, applying equal punishment across sexes (Naqvi, 1968: 159). Whether sentencing was gender-equitable in practice remains unclear, suggesting potential legal inconsistencies despite formal parity.

Kasravi too advocated for stringent measures to protect future generations, opposing procreation by individuals with hereditary diseases and proposing penalties for such unions (Regan, 1985: 70). Kasravi and Taj shared a belief in education as a preventative mechanism against marital incompatibility, emphasising its role in cultivating empathy, responsibility, and mutual respect (Regan, 1985: 69). Yet while reformist discourses gestured towards equality, the gendered regulation of bodies and behaviours persisted, revealing the state's investment in maintaining patriarchal control under the guise of national improvement.

Equality and Matrimony

Although legislative acts were introduced to formalise family structures, the rights granted to women remained minimal, tightly circumscribed by a set of stringent conditions. The issue of child marriage, in particular, served as a flashpoint for feminist intervention. Divergent approaches emerged among women's groups, reflecting broader questions about strategy, identity, and the evolving role of women in society. Despite the limited size and organisational reach of the Iranian women's movement, Colliver-Rice (1923: 274) observed that its significance lay less in its structure and more in the critical awareness it generated about women's subordinate status and their collective aspirations for progress—an observation that equally applies to the Egyptian context.

Yet, a central and complex question arises: why did elite figures such as Huda Sha'rawi—founder of *Al-Ittihād Al-Nisā'ī Al-Miṣrī*—align themselves with the concept of the 'Western-style nuclear family?' (Fay, 2003: 77). The reforms advocated by Huda and *Al-Ittihād Al-Nisā'ī Al-Miṣrī* did not merely aim to emulate Western domestic models; rather, they represented an attempt to recalibrate the 'patriarchal bargain' within the ideological and institutional architecture of the modern

Egyptian nation-state (Fay, 2003: 92). With the ratification of the 1923 Constitution, a new vision of Egypt began to coalesce—one shaped by European-educated legal elites and infused with cultural imports from the West. While Islam remained enshrined as the state religion, the emerging political order bore the imprint of secularism, suggesting that Egypt, although officially Islamic, could not be fully characterised as a religious state.

Throughout the early decades of the twentieth century, customary practices—particularly arranged marriages—continued to dominate, with legal interventions only gradually imposing age limits on marriage. Despite these regulations, traditional mechanisms such as *mahr* and *wali* retained their centrality, reinforcing patriarchal authority over women's autonomy. Even as marriage rates declined, women who did marry remained entangled in structural inequalities both within the private sphere and throughout the marriage process itself.

By contrast, Iran's family laws, rooted in *Šiʿeh-yi Ithnā ʿAshari* jurisprudence, underwent formal codification through a series of legislative enactments between 1928 and 1935. Civil and marriage laws, drafted by the *Majles*, were nonetheless consistent with *Sharīʿa* (Vatandoust, 1985: 114). Within this legal framework, reforms introduced under *Reza Šah* granted women limited grounds for divorce—such as the right to leave a husband who refused monogamy—and required men to disclose existing marriages before entering into a new one. Although child marriage appeared to be legally addressed through a prohibition against marrying individuals who had not yet reached puberty, this reform proved largely symbolic, effectively nullifying the law's protective intent (Sanasarian, 1982: 61).

While these reforms nominally engaged with feminist demands, *Reza Šah* modernising agenda prioritised visible, symbolic transformations—such as the banning of the veil—over substantive legal equity. His emphasis on Western dress codes and the visibility of women in public life deflected attention from enduring gender disparities in matrimonial law. As Sanasarian (1982: 65–66) astutely notes, the preoccupation with unveiling functioned as a political spectacle, obscuring the fact that many women—particularly those already married and embedded in familial structures—remained far more concerned with educational access, legal protection, and economic security than with the adoption of European fashion.

This disjuncture between state-imposed 'secular' modernity and women's lived realities was also captured by Colliver-Rice (1923: 91), who questioned how Iranian men could assume the roles of patriotic leaders while their mothers remained uneducated and excluded from the public sphere. Her commentary underscores the intrinsic link between the domestic and political realms: when women are denied intellectual development and civic engagement, the nation's capacity for progress is inevitably stunted.

In Egypt, women's visibility increased marginally after the 1919 revolution, but the underlying gender hierarchy remained firmly in place. As Botman (1991: 107) observes, women continued to be conceptualised as possessions within a male-dominated social order—an assessment equally relevant in the Iranian context, where legal and cultural norms persistently framed female agency as contingent upon male authority.

Dissolution of a Marriage

Though both men and women were legally able to initiate divorce, the conditions under which women could do so were significantly restricted. Grounds such as polygamy, financial neglect, prolonged absence, incarceration, or abuse served not as avenues of liberation but as tightly drawn thresholds that women were required to cross before the law permitted their exit from marriage. As such, women found themselves navigating a legal and familial terrain where the formal availability of rights was continually tempered by the patriarchal architecture that governed both public and private life. That divorce might be wielded as a male prerogative remained a persistent assumption, but evidence from legal documents and personal narratives complicates this notion. The dissolution of marriage, whether through divorce or death, is revealed not only as a personal rupture but as a moment wherein gendered hierarchies are both enacted and resisted.

In *Gender Equality, Matrimony and Secularism in Egypt and Iran*, this dynamic is foregrounded through case studies that illustrate how women's limited agency in ending marriages was shaped not merely by Islamic law, but also by the emerging secular legal codes born out of colonial influence. The book also disrupts any notion of unbounded male autonomy, highlighting the subtle constraints placed on men by state interests and shifting legal paradigms. Control over the termination

S. Louden-Cooke, *Gender Equality, Matrimony and Secularism in Egypt and Iran: A Comparative Exploration of Early Twentieth-Century Family Law*, Middle East Today,
https://doi.org/10.1007/978-3-032-00846-6_5

of marriage, it becomes clear, was not simply about individual will, but about the shaping of national identities through legal and familial policy.

Perceptions of divorce in Muslim-majority societies often frame it as a disciplinary tool, responding to a woman's supposed failure to remain physically appealing, compliant, or reproductively successful—particularly in failing to bear sons (Colliver-Rice, 1923: 91). A woman suggesting divorce might find herself denied her *mahr*, the payment due upon the formalisation of divorce *by him*, unless she could prove that her husband had violated contractual terms. While these stipulations could serve as safeguards, their enforcement rested on the same patriarchal logic that made divorce an exercise in male authority.

The significance of contractual stipulations is vividly illustrated in the life of Huda, whose mother, prior to her marriage, had insisted that Huda would be her husband's sole wife—a condition later betrayed. On learning of his polygamy, Huda left Ali and returned to her mother's home (Fay, 2003: 94), remaining separated from him for seven years (Sharawi Lanfranchi, 2012: 29). Notably, this act of self-determination preceded her engagement with European feminists such as Eugénie Le Brun[1] and thus cannot be dismissed as the product of Western influence. Instead, it gestures towards an indigenous feminist consciousness shaped by family dynamics, individual experience, and a passion for learning (Fay, 2003: 94). Consequently, Fay (2003) seeks to understand the conditions that altered Huda's perceptions of the family structure.

Though Huda eventually reunited with Ali at the age of twenty-two, her earlier withdrawal reveals both an assertion of contractual rights and a refusal to accept betrayal in silence. Yet, as Badran (in Shaarawi, 1987: 18) observes, such actions were far from typical among young women of the time. The qualifier 'young' is telling; it suggests a generational or experiential threshold after which such resistance may have become more socially (un)acceptable. Even so, Huda's temporary separation marks a fissure in the normative family narrative and reflects the development of a distinctly personal awareness of marital rights.

Taj's experience offers a parallel yet distinct challenge to male-dominated divorce norms. Despite the absence of formal stipulations, Taj narrates her divorce in the first person (Taj, n.d./2003: 216), with

[1] Eugenie Le Brun was the wife of Husain Rushdi Pasha. Born in France and later marrying an Egyptian man, Eugenie was a great influence in Huda's life, was prominent in Egyptian feminist politics, and was a prominent salon host.

Amanat (in al-Sultana/Vanzan & Neshati, n.d./2003: 217) also recognising, suggesting a female-voiced agency that legal records may not fully endorse. Though the formal right to finalise divorce belonged to men, these accounts disturb the clarity of that boundary. Both Taj and Huda, in their own ways, exerted influence over the course of their marriages, defying expectations and resisting the roles they were assigned. In both cases, their narratives centre on personal authority rather than legal permission.

Sattareh (1993: 136), however, later reflects on *Reza Šah* performative reforms, particularly his desire to 'create the appearance of emancipation'. Policies associated with secular modernity, such as the veneer of gender equality in legal frameworks, served more to embellish the state's modernist credentials than to enact genuine structural change. Beneath this superficial transformation, patriarchal norms remained deeply entrenched, revealing that legal reforms were often curated symbols of state identity rather than vehicles for substantive gender justice, with a secular façade presenting a 'modernised' state whose private sphere remained embedded in religious frameworks. The desire to 'modernise the state', however, did result in increasingly secular attitudes towards the paradigms of everyday life.

Initiating Divorce

The promulgation of Egyptian Law 24/1920 marked the early stirrings of reform within family law, granting women conditional grounds for divorce based on financial incapacity or incurable illness of the husband (Sadiqi & Ennaji, 2011: 135). While this legislative development appeared to soften the rigidity of previous divorce restrictions, it nevertheless reasserted the gendered asymmetries embedded in marital frameworks. The criteria required to substantiate such claims—along with the burden of evidentiary proof—ensured that masculine dominance in the legal construction of marriage remained largely intact. A similar codification occurred in Iran with the 1928 Civil Code, notably in Sections 1120–1142 (Naqvi, 1968b: 358), where the boundaries of permissible female agency were cautiously delineated.

Section 1121 of Iran's Civil Code stipulated that either spouse could revoke a marriage in the event of confirmed insanity, 'whether permanent or intermittent' (Naqvi, 1968b: 358). The ambiguity of such phrasing—eschewing clarity on the duration or recurrence of the condition—positioned judicial discretion as a gatekeeper of female recourse. While both male and female impairments were outlined, the framing remained distinctly asymmetrical. Imperfections impeding male conjugal duties were addressed specifically; those attributed to women were couched in broader, less technical language. The list of female 'blemishes' was not only twice as long but also predominantly defined by visual or functional deformities, including black and white leprosy, vaginal obstructions, and blindness—each serving to render the female body a site of juridical scrutiny and social anxiety (Naqvi, 1968b: 358; Taleghany, 1995: 164).

By contrast, the grounds available to women were narrowly confined: impotence, eunuchism, and penile amputation, and even then, a wife had to endure a waiting period of one year after impotency occurred in order to appeal to the judiciary before divorce proceedings could commence (Naqvi, 1968b: 358; Taleghany, 1995: 163). No such latency applied to male claimants. Nor did men require judicial authorisation for revocation, and the doubling of the number of female 'blemishes', underscores once more the ease with which male agency operated in the dissolution of marriage. The legal text, couched in ostensibly secular language, nevertheless drew upon deeply entrenched Qur'anic prescriptions, thereby reinforcing a religious/secular dialectic rather than circumventing it.

Further elaboration came in Section 1124, which clarified that such conditions only entitled men to annul the marriage if they predated its formalisation (Naqvi, 1968b: 359). Section 1125 afforded women slightly broader parameters, allowing revocation on grounds of impotence or insanity even if these emerged post-nuptially. However, these provisions were quickly circumscribed again in Section 1126, which rendered prior knowledge of any defect disqualifying. Section 1127 permitted a woman to refuse intercourse with a husband afflicted by a venereal disease without forfeiting maintenance (Naqvi, 1968b: 359), illustrating how bodily health was central to juridico-religious assessments of marital viability and the broader imperative of preserving a 'healthy' family unit. The family, articulated in secular language yet embedded within a religious framework, becomes a site where the illusion of state-religion separation is carefully presented. Beneath this secular façade, the entanglement of religious authority and political power quietly persists.

Sections 1129 and 1130 introduced further provisions: if a man failed to fulfil his marital duties—whether through financial neglect, violence, or illness—a wife could appeal to the *qāḍī* (قَاضِي; judge) for a compelled divorce (Naqvi, 1968b: 359; Taleghany, 1995: 164–165). The language here was revealing. A woman did not divorce; she requested permission for her husband to be 'compelled' into initiating the divorce. Legal recognition of her suffering or instability was thus contingent on male compliance or judicial intercession. Moreover, Section 1120 clarified that only husbands could unilaterally dissolve permanent marriages, while *sigheh* could be ended by the husband relinquishing the remaining time (Naqvi, 1968b: 358). These regulatory contours suggest not just a legal gender hierarchy but also a structural mistrust of female autonomy in matters of marital termination.

The Egyptian context shared some of these dynamics. The right for women to sue for divorce on grounds of *darar* (harm or mistreatment) was recognised in 1921, with judicial divorce being possible by 1929 if reconciliation failed (Kholoussy, 2010: 97). Yet, even prior to this, repudiation had been prohibited (Badran, 1991: 76, cited in Sadiqi & Ennaji, 2011: 135), a move which, while ostensibly progressive, also served to curtail avenues of separation altogether. Reforms addressed minimum marriage ages and diminished the requirement for parental consent, but the deep entanglement of religious tenets and secular language meant that gendered divisions and assumptions remained largely unchallenged.

Law 25/1929 further revised the Egyptian Personal Status framework. Chapter 2 addressed marital discord and divorce resulting from harm to the wife; with Article 6 authorising a woman to seek divorce if her husband's conduct was demonstrably damaging (The Egyptian Gazette, 1929: 4). If the *qāḍī* deemed reconciliation unfeasible and credible evidence was presented, *ṭalāqun bā'inun* (طَلَاقٌ بَائِنٌ; irrevocable divorce) could be issued. Rejected or weak claims were sent to arbitrators—one from each family—whose negotiations determined the next steps (Articles 7–10), and ultimately, the *qāḍī* was bound by their judgement (Article 11). Though overt religious references were absent, the embedded role of the *qāḍī* ensured the enduring influence of religious authority.

Women's right to divorce based on the husband's absence for a year or more, regardless of his financial provision, further reinforced the importance of familial proximity over material sufficiency (Article 12, The Egyptian Gazette, 1929: 4). If the absent husband could be contacted, he was given a deadline to return or grant a divorce; otherwise, the divorce proceeded without delay (Articles 13–14). Imprisonment for three years or more similarly enabled a woman to seek divorce after a one-year waiting period. Religious undertones, subtly present in these provisions, suggest that women's legal status remained contingent on patriarchal interpretations of morality and order. Notably, these references became less pronounced in discussions of male divorce, implying a more secular approach to male rights.

Articles 21 and 22 addressed the presumption of death, allowing a woman to be declared a widow if her husband had disappeared under life-threatening circumstances and four years had passed. The *qāḍī* decision was preceded by exhaustive inquiries, and any such declaration required the widow to observe *iddet el wafat*, with inheritance being divided among his surviving heirs on the date of decision, reinforcing religious norms even in legal determinations (The Egyptian Gazette, 1929: 4). Meanwhile, repudiation was restricted under duress, signalling growing concern with both procedural fairness and reputational legitimacy (Sadiqi & Ennaji, 2011: 135).

In contrast to Egypt, Iran's legal architecture afforded greater recognition to contractual stipulations. Sections 1128 and 1131 allowed for revocation where the marriage contract misrepresented one party's qualities, provided action was taken upon discovery (Naqvi, 1968b: 359–360). Section 1119 and the Marriage Act further empowered women, though only those possessing a power of attorney, which was to be proven by a certificate, to repudiate themselves if their husbands breached agreed-upon terms (Naqvi, 1968a: 159; Taleghany, 1995: 163; Vatandoust, 1985: 116). Egypt, while lacking formal recognition of such clauses, saw their growing informal legitimacy, reflecting the interplay between custom and codified law.

The Iranian Civil Code also addressed general divorce procedures. Men could unilaterally divorce, subject only to the presence of two male witnesses or an authorised agent, and it was contingent on mental stability and genuine intent (Naqvi, 1967: 242; 1968b: 359). A guardian could act on behalf of mentally unfit men, underscoring the patriarchal continuity even in incapacitation. Divorce was restricted to permanent marriages, with temporary unions dissolved through renunciation. Even the physical state of the female body—menstruation, for instance—could invalidate a divorce unless certain conditions applied (Naqvi, 1968b: 360; Taleghany, 1995: 166). In this way, the female body became a site of legal and religious convergence, a node where juridical control, religious symbolism, and biopolitical governance intersected, further emphasising the absence of female agency experienced by some women.

The early twentieth century in Egypt witnessed an upsurge in feminist consciousness and public discourse surrounding secularism. While some secular groups challenged the state's reading of Islam rather than the religion itself, male control over divorce and paternal authority in marriage arrangements faced increasing contestation. Paternal annulments could be achieved by proving the groom's 'inferior social status', revealing that jurisdiction over marriage dissolution extended beyond husbands and *qāḍī* (Kholoussy, 2010: 112, 114). Class, therefore, emerged as a determinant of marital positioning, weaving a complex fabric in which patriarchal and socio-economic hierarchies overlapped.

Ultimately, the apparent move towards gender parity in both Egyptian and Iranian legal systems belied the structural rigidity beneath. Egypt's lack of recognised stipulations and Iran's onerous procedural requirements signal a resistance to female-initiated divorce cloaked in the language of reform. While women's legal standing saw incremental advancement, their rights remained tightly circumscribed within a patriarchal architecture. The legal vocabulary may have adopted secular idioms, yet its referents remained religious, reinforcing the hybridised nature of legal modernity in Muslim-majority contexts. The cases of Huda and Taj—though predating these reforms—foreshadowed many of the legal and cultural debates that would come to define women's marital rights. Their stories, albeit exceptional, offer glimpses of evolving self-awareness and resistance, later absorbed and codified within legal systems that continued to oscillate between religious authority and secular presentation.

Types of Divorce

Within Islamic jurisprudence, divorce manifests in multiple forms, reflecting the doctrinal divergence between Sunni and Shiʿi legal traditions. The Sunni schools recognise two principal types of *ṭalāq*. *Ṭalāq* in conformity with the *Sunna* is deemed valid after the observance of *al-ʿIddah*—a legally mandated waiting period—or, in cases of pregnancy, post-childbirth. Even when the repudiation is pronounced once or thrice over as many months, the severance remains *rājʿah* (رَاجِعَة; revocable), enabling the husband to reclaim the marriage within the confines of *al-ʿIddah* (Coulson & Hinchcliffe, 1978: 42–43). The apparent leniency of this process, however, positions women in a space of temporal vulnerability, where dissolution is suspended and potentially revoked at the husband's discretion, illustrating an alternative avenue through which *interpersonal power-over* can be explored.

In contrast, *ṭalāq al-bid'a*—an innovation lacking in religious legitimacy but not in legal efficacy—has emerged as the most widely practised form of divorce (Coulson & Hinchcliffe, 1978: 43). This method requires three consecutive pronouncements in one sitting and results in an immediate and irrevocable termination of the marriage. The woman, however, is not permitted to remarry her former husband unless she first marries and consummates a union with another man—thus rendering her body a conduit through which legal requirements are achieved. This practice, while effective, is morally censured, and its legitimacy is rejected entirely by *Ši'eh-yi Ithnā 'Ashari* (Coulson & Hinchcliffe, 1978: 43).

The *Shi'i* school imposes a more exacting standard: specific criteria must be fulfilled, accurate [Arabic] pronouncements made, and *al-'Iddah* duly observed for a divorce to be legally recognised (Ferdows, 1985: 28). Sunni jurisprudence, by comparison, offers a less formalised process, with the exception of *al-'Iddah* as a shared obligation (Ferdows, 1985: 28). Ferdows (1985: 27), interpreting Mernissi, suggests that the persistence of *khul'* and *tamlik* divorces constitutes a faint echo of pre-Islamic marital systems—ones in which women exercised greater sexual autonomy and more symmetrical rights of dissolution. The contemporary codification of these practices, then, reflects not merely religious doctrine but also an evolving relationship between family regulation and state-sanctioned religion, wherein secularism functions as a discursive tool to critique interpretation rather than dismantle patriarchal authority.

The Egyptian Draft Law of 1929 defines *ṭalāq* as the denial of a marriage contract, or refusal to uphold spousal duties by the husband. The articles are precise in their effort to mitigate abusive or impulsive repudiation:

> Article 1.—Repudiation (of a wife by a husband) made in a state of drunkenness or under constrains is invalid.
>
> Article 2.—Conditional repudiation, used as a means of constraining the wife to do or not to do certain acts is invalid.
>
> Article 3.—A single repudiation remains a single repudiation even though accompanied by words or gestures aiming at giving it a multiple or threefold significance.
>
> Article 4.—A formula of repudiation which is ambiguously worded is only valid as a repudiation providing the intent to repudiate is clearly established.

> Article 5.—Every repudiation is "Radjii" or revocable, except repudiation pronounced for the third time (three-fold repudiation); repudiation prior to the consummation of marriage, repudiation in exchange for compensation, and the repudiation considered as "Bains" or irrevocable by the present Law and by Law No. 25 of 1920.
>
> (The Egyptian Gazette, 12 March 1929: 4)

These reforms curbed some of the more arbitrary and coercive expressions of male power, ensuring that divorce could no longer be executed under duress or intoxication. Yet these limitations did not fundamentally challenge the asymmetrical structure of divorce itself. The husband remained the sole actor in initiating *ṭalāq*; the wife's legal standing, although somewhat protected, remained passive. What was achieved was a procedural insulation, not equality.

This patriarchal logic was further reinforced by Iran's Civil Code. Articles 1143–1155 (Naqvi, 1968b: 361) outlined the recognised forms of divorce. A marriage could be dissolved through *khulʿ* or *mubārāt* only if the wife waived financial claims. *Khulʿ* was predicated on the wife's declared aversion to her husband, involving compensation—typically equal to or exceeding the dower—paid to the husband. *Mubārāt*, by contrast, was a mutual dissolution grounded in shared animosity, but the compensation could not exceed the dower (Naqvi, 1968b: 361; Taleghany, 1995: 167). Where consummation had not occurred or where the wife could no longer bear children, the revocability of divorce was similarly rescinded. Naqvi (1967: 242) notes that the formalisation of *ṭalāqun bā'inun* was intended, in part, to protect women from the instability of *rājʿah* divorce, where a husband might retract his repudiation at any point during *al-ʿIddah*. These legal mechanisms, while ostensibly protective, underscored the centrality of male control and religious sanction in the governance of marital dissolution.

In practice, Egyptian law recognised multiple forms of *ṭalāq*, yet if a woman sought to initiate separation, *taṭlīq* (تَطْلِيق; divorce by a third party)—a judicial mechanism in which the *qāḍī* appointed male arbitrators to evaluate the case. This procedural detour preserved *ṭalāq* as a male prerogative, situating women's legal recourse within male-dominated religious and familial frameworks. Divorce classifications—revocable, minor irrevocable, and major irrevocable—continued to reflect a gendered legal imagination. In *rājʿah* divorce, the husband could unilaterally restore the marriage during *al-ʿIddah*, without the wife's consent or the need for a new contract (NWRO, n.d.: 47). Minor irrevocable divorce required a new marriage contract and *mahr* if reconciliation occurred, but only with the wife's consent. Major irrevocable divorce, meanwhile, prohibited reconciliation altogether unless the woman had remarried and the new marriage had ended—effectively transforming the female body into a juridical threshold through which male power was both relinquished and potentially reclaimed (NWRO, n.d.: 47).

Women's grounds for requesting judicial divorce included imprisonment, harm, illness, polygamy, and prolonged absence (NWRO, n.d.: 48–50). Nonetheless, such rights often remained aspirational; the legal structure continued to situate marriage and its dissolution within a male-controlled domain. The Hanafi school, dominant in Egypt since the Ottoman era, entrenched this asymmetry through its interpretive authority (Shaham, 1999: 463). The retention of an Islamic legal framework for family law further reinforced the enduring entanglement between religion, the family, and the state.

Whereas divorce was the normative pathway for separation, annulment emerged as an alternative, though its applicability hinged on the presence of witnesses during the marriage ceremony. In the contentious case of mixed marriages, the validity of union and dissolution became further entangled in issues of religion and colonial authority. Muslim men could legally marry non-Muslim women, but such arrangements exposed deep legal fissures, particularly when the validity of the union was contested. A 1927 memorandum from the Acting First Secretary clarified that:

> …2. 'Article 120 of the Code du Statut Personnel recognizes the validity of a marriage between a Mohammedan and a Christian woman, provided that there are two Christian witnesses to the wedding. But, although these witnesses can bind the Christian woman, their testimony is valueless against the Mohammedan man. It seems to follow from this, that in a case such as the present where the Mohammedan man denies the validity of the marriage, there will be no witness to prove it, and, therefore, under Article 134 (4) it will be null and void, as being a marriage contracted without witnesses.
>
> …3…By Article 217 the husband alone has the right of repudiation. Divorce can apparently be obtained by mutual consent…
>
> (TNA, FO 141/792/4)

These provisions betray a legal order in which non-Muslim women were afforded minimal protection. Their testimony lacked the evidentiary status afforded to Muslim men, and the requirement for Christian witnesses—without equivalent stipulations for Muslim testimony—suggests a hierarchy in which both non-Muslim men and (Muslim) women were juridically subordinate, echoing traditional Islamic evidentiary standards that value a woman's testimony as half that of a man. The asymmetry here is apparent, with Muslim men possessing the authority to dissolve mixed marriages unilaterally, while their partners were structurally disenfranchised. This framework illustrates not only the patriarchal logic of personal status law but also its colonial entanglements, wherein legal protections for (non-Muslim) women were curtailed by the intersection of gender, religion, and empire.

Polygamy and Temporary Marriage

In Western discourse, polygamy is often regarded as the most prominent and contentious feature of Islamic marriage (Ferdows, 1985: 19). The homogeneity of its interpretation among Sunni and Shi'i Muslims stems from the foundational text of *sūrah* 4:3 of the Qur'an, which permits men to marry up to four wives, but only under specific conditions and without encouragement of the practice (Ferdows, 1985: 19). Sunni and Shi'i scholars justify polygamy as a social safeguard against 'spinsterhood' and as a means for men to father children in cases of female infertility without resorting to divorce (Lari, 1979: 115 cited in Ferdows, 1985: 20). This justification reflects broader anxieties about female-to-male birth ratios, male mortality from war, reproductive restrictions on women, and economic hardships that limit women's marital prospects (Lari, 1979: 114 cited in Ferdows, 1985: 20).

Despite controversies over the absence of monogamy, both Egyptian and Iranian legal systems preserved men's right to multiple wives, even as emerging feminist voices in these countries challenged the practice. Iranian law also permitted *sigheh* with predetermined durations which could be hours to decades, introducing a contractual element that further entrenched male dominance and arguably destabilised familial structures more than polygamy itself.

Polygamous Relations

In Egypt, polygamy remained largely unregulated except for Article 11 of Law No. 25/1929, which granted women the right to petition for divorce if a husband's additional marriage caused physical or moral harm, making cohabitation impossible (NWRO, n.d.: 60). Yet this right was limited by patriarchal constraints, with the (first) wife having to apply within one year of learning of the new marriage, while also having to provide proof of unresolvable issues, and the *qāḍī* retaining authority to attempt reconciliation, with final divorce decisions remaining male-dominated (Talhami, 1996: 115). The law's incremental concession permitted women to request divorce but preserved male jurisdiction over its approval, thereby reinforcing patriarchal family structures and the inseparability of religion and state in Egypt's political sphere, thus evidencing the absence of this relationship in Egyptian secularism.

Iranian family law similarly offered women conditional divorce rights if their husbands failed to provide maintenance, subjected them to maltreatment, endangered their lives, or took another wife[2] (Section 119, Iranian Civil Code in Naqvi, 1968a: 157–158; Taleghany, 1995: 163). However, the process required judicial approval, underscoring divorce as a male-controlled institution and reflecting how family law reproduced broader social power hierarchies (Urry, 2011: 104–105). Betrothed men were also legally obliged to disclose existing marriages on the 'marriage deed', and failure to do so invited prosecution if the wife filed a complaint (Sections 6 and 7, Marriage Act, Naqvi, 1968a: 159). While multiple wives were generally permissible, polygamy generated instability and uncertainty among wives, and was thus usually considered detrimental to family unit (Colliver-Rice, 1923: 51).

Despite feminist critiques, personal narratives complicate this picture. Sattareh recalls her father's polygamous marriages as rooted in religious devotion, justified morally and legally when his first wife, Ezzatdoleh, could no longer bear children or fulfil conjugal duties (Farman Farmaian, 1993: 54). She also recalls harmonious relations among wives, highlighting how wealth and social status mediated the practice, allowing deviation from the four-wife limit set by Islamic law (Coulson & Hinchcliffe, 1978: 40). Among *Šiʿeh-yi Ithnā ʿAshari*, no permission is needed from current wives for further marriages, nor are there limits on *sigheh* (Coulson & Hinchcliffe, 1978: 40).

[2] The words 'whenever a husband marries another woman' were removed from Section 4 of the Marriage Act, thus revoking the woman's right to divorce her husband should the relationship become polygamous as was previously afforded to her in the Civil Code (Naqvi, 1968a: 131).

In Egypt, concerns also arose about non-Egyptian women in mixed marriages enduring stresses from polygamous relations. A 1931 letter from the Society for the Overseas Settlement of British Women (TNA, FO 141/792) expresses incredulity that women could stipulate in marriage contracts a ban on their husbands taking additional wives, revealing colonial attitudes of control and a perception of Islamic marriage as an inferior, polygamy-defined institution.

5/1/31

Dear Sir,

I was interested to see in Saturday's "Times" the enclosed paragraph. I shall be interested to know whether you can find out if it really is law that a wife can stipulate in marriage contract that the man should not marry anyone else.

In paragraph 21 of the enclosed with regard to marriage laws, it does not give information, and in interviewing any woman who is bent on marrying a Mohammedan, we could advise her to get this kind of contract if it really would be legal in Egypt.

Yours Faithfully
E.S. Nicholas

(TNA, FO 141/792)

Hatem (1989: 186) traces polygamy's origins to pre-Islamic traditions, adopted into Islamic law. Islamist defenders assert that polygamy cannot be considered harmful to the first wife given its *Sharīʿah* sanction (Talhami, 1996: 115). Yet the Qur'anic injunction in *Sūrah* 4:3 cautions men to marry only one woman if they fear injustice, reflecting ethical limits to the practice (Ali, 2000: 60).

Egypt's 1929 law allowing divorce petitions on grounds of 'harm' from successive marriages echoes this principle but retains male judicial authority over divorce, underscoring the symbolic rather than substantive nature of women's rights. The law's limited reforms emerged in response to feminist demands by groups such as *Al-Ittihād Al-Nisāʾī Al-Miṣrī*, who sought broader equality, including restrictions on male unilateral divorce and the abolition of polygamy (Talhami, 1996: 11).

In Iran, reforms under Reza Khan (1926–1940) similarly balanced modernist pressures with preserving patriarchal norms. These legal changes reveal the façade of secular reform for the benefit of an international audience, while traditional religious-patriarchal structures remained embedded in family law, highlighting the incomplete secularisation, with Iran's *internal* secularism focussing on externally visible aspects of society as determined by Reza Khan's modernisation project, and Egypt's colonially introduced *external* secularism engaging only with aspects of society where colonial relationships were most prominent.

An Expiration Date

Marriage stands as a fundamental institution through which patriarchal power structures are both expressed and maintained (Walters, 2011: 18). This dynamic becomes particularly evident when examining the practice of *sigheh*, which remained legally sanctioned in Iran but was absent from Egyptian law. Ferdows (1985: 22) traces *sigheh* back to pre-Islamic customs, where both men and women exercised relative autonomy in selecting partners and contracting marriages without paternal interference. Despite this apparent liberalism in its formation, *sigheh* was frequently criticised and condemned as tantamount to prostitution, a judgement stemming from the abuses associated with the practice (Ferdows, 1985: 22). Within Shi'i Islam, *sigheh* retains its legal status, justified as a mechanism to curb illicit sexual behaviour such as adultery (Ferdows, 1985: 22). Sunni Islam, however, rejects this,[3] citing the revocation of its permissibility by a tradition recorded in Muslim's Sahih concerning *sūrah* 4:25 (Ferdows, 1985: 23). This divergence between Sunni and Shi'i interpretations not only explains the legal status of sigheh in Iran during this era, but also highlights how doctrinal differences foster distinct cultural practices, shaping varying conceptions of what is deemed 'suitable' within marriage.

The Shi'i Fiqh, and subsequently, Iranian law, placed no explicit limits on the number of temporary wives a man might contract, so long as he possessed the financial means and physical capacity to ensure equitable treatment (Naqvi, 1967: 245–246). While unrestricted in quantity, *sigheh* nonetheless imposed requirements akin to those found in polygamous unions, underscoring shared concerns around economic and emotional responsibilities. Sections 1075–1077 of the Iranian Civil Code detailed these provisions, defining a temporary marriage as valid only when explicitly limited by a time-bound contract, which could range 'from an hour to ninety years' (Sanasarian, 1982: 13). Crucially,

[3] In Arabic, temporary marriage translates to Irfiyy (يفرع). In Persian Ezdevaje movaqqat (تقوم جاودز) is also used, and Moteh/motah (هعتم) is often used by jurists.

only men retained the right to hold multiple temporary spouses simultaneously, reinforcing the patriarchal framework within which marriage operates. This gendered limitation mirrors the restrictions on polygamy and starkly exposes the absence of gender parity, signalling how women's roles within family law remain subordinate and contingent, and at times, disposable.

In terms of legal rights, *sigheh* carried distinct stipulations regarding inheritance and dower. Neither spouse could claim inheritance from the other, and the male's obligation for financial maintenance ceased at the conclusion of the contract (Ferdows, 1985: 23; Naqvi, 1968a: 153). Yet, children born within these temporary unions were granted financial rights comparable to those born from permanent marriages, including entitlement to support and inheritance (Ferdows, 1985: 22). This dichotomy, excluding women from sustained legal and economic protection while safeguarding children's rights, highlights the transactional and utilitarian nature of *sigheh*.

The social ramifications for women involved in *sigheh* proved profound. Though legally recognised as 'real wives', their social standing closely resembled that of slave concubines, particularly reflected in the reduced duration of their *al-'Iddah*—the waiting period following the end of the marriage—lasting only half as long as that of women exiting permanent marriages (Ferdows, 1985: 23). Such disparities illuminate not only the divergent interpretations and applications of temporary marriage but also the enduring impact on women's lives long after these unions dissolve. Central to these issues is the ease with which men could enter and exit marriages of indeterminate length, thereby reinforcing male dominance and control within the institution, and underscoring the precariousness of women's social and legal positions in such arrangements.

Financial Concerns: Maintenance, Alimony, and Inheritance

The family, as a nexus of patriarchal power, reaches beyond marriage and gender roles into the ostensibly 'private' economic domain. Here, financial obligations fall squarely upon the husband, whose wealth not only dictates the mahr but also funds the maintenance of his wife and children. It is on this financial footing that a man's capacity to sustain a polygamous household is assessed. Against this backdrop of patriarchal family law and economic control, this section interrogates women's financial rights upon the dissolution of marriage; whether through divorce or widowhood.

Maintenance and Alimony

Following divorce, women could claim any unpaid *mahr*, with maintenance extending throughout the *al-ʿIddah* period; thereafter, they retained the right to seek ongoing financial support (Coulson & Hinchcliffe, 1978: 43). Islamic legal schools converge on the principle that maintenance continues beyond *al-ʿIddah* in *rājʿah* divorces, yet diverge on *ṭalāqun bāʾinun*. The Hanafī school alone permits extended maintenance regardless, while others restrict it to pregnant women (Coulson & Hinchcliffe, 1978: 43).

Shiʾi jurisprudence offers a distinct approach to financial aspects of divorce, notably with khul and faskh. Khul divorce allows women to seek separation provided they relinquish mahr and maintenance rights during *al-ʿIddah* (Ferdows, 1985: 26). Conversely, faskh remains revocable, allowing husbands to reclaim their wives—an extension of patriarchal prerogative justified by Shi'i scholars as a natural male right rooted in female vulnerability and the family's fragile cohesion (Ferdows, 1985: 27).

Financial concerns in marital dissolution span four areas: mahr, maintenance, alimony, and inheritance. Egyptian Law 25/1920, influenced by more permissive Maliki Shafi'i school, broadened divorce grounds to include husband's failure to provide, disappearance, and illness, reflecting a modest liberalising shift (Kholoussy, 2010: 93). *Al-ʿIddah* for women not pregnant or breastfeeding was capped at one year, irrespective of menstruation (Kholoussy, 2010: 89).

Alimony provisions, codified in this chapter (The Egyptian Gazette,12 March 1929: 4), hinged on male wealth, ignoring women's economic status. Payments lasted no longer than twelve months, underscoring male financial responsibility during *al-ʿIddah* irrespective of *ṭalāq* (Articles 16 and 17). The law's openness to multiple Islamic interpretations reflects a relatively less restrictive stance within other schools.

Iran's Civil Code similarly mandated maintenance for permanent marriages, including clothing, food, lodging, and household items commensurate with the wife's accustomed standard (Sections 1106 and 1107 in

Naqvi, 1968a: 156; Taleghany, 1995: 161). Wives refusing marital duties could lose maintenance barring legal justification, while widows received no maintenance during their *al-ʿIddah* (Sections 1108–1110 in Naqvi, 1968a: 156). Moreover, maintenance obligations were enforceable through courts if men defaulted, though *sigheh* lacked such requirements unless contractually specified (Sections 1111 and 1113 in Naqvi, 1968a: 156–157). Husbands also controlled accommodation choices unless delegated to wives, and should his conduct threaten the her, she was entitled to separate housing, with courts adjudicating disputes over suitable accommodation (Sections 1114–1116 in Naqvi, 1968a: 157). The Marriage Act's enactment did, however, remove the qualifier 'permanent marriage', extending male maintenance duties to all marriages and empowering courts to grant religious sanction for divorce if maintenance obligations were unmet (Section 1112 in Naqvi, 1968a: 131–132).

The ninth book of Iranian law explicitly detailed maintenance responsibilities. Section 1199 assigned male accountability for child maintenance, cascading to the paternal grandfather if necessary. Absent paternal, male kin resulted in the wife's family assuming responsibility (Naqvi, 1968b: 282). Moreover, the wife's entitlement to maintenance took precedence over other beneficiaries, who could only claim future payments, thus reinforcing her primary financial priority in legal disputes (Sections 1203, 1205–1206 in Naqvi, 1968b: 283).

Post-divorce child affiliation depended on precise temporal criteria related to birth and sexual intercourse—the child's birth was no more than ten months after divorce and that sex had occurred less than half a year or more than ten months prior to child birth (Section 1159 in Naqvi, 1968b: 284). These rules persisted even if the woman remarried (Section 1160 in Naqvi, 1968b: 284), reaffirming the gendered economic hierarchy that positions men as primary financial providers, marginalising women within the private sphere.

This economic framework highlights the embedded patriarchy within family law and exposes the limits placed on women's autonomy in financial matters. Secularism, though rhetorically present, remains overshadowed by the state's intertwining of religion and family identity—perhaps a strategic posture resisting colonial influences. While religion continues to shape state and family relations, policy language reveals a tentative separation of religion and politics, rather than a full secular divorce from religious authority.

Inheritance

Inheritance laws starkly illuminate gender inequality, with women consistently receiving substantially smaller shares than their male relatives. Ferdows (1985: 24) identifies these laws as among the most defining features distinguishing *Ši'eh-yi Ithnā 'Ashari* from Sunni jurisprudence, noting that Shi'i law grounds inheritance primarily in blood relations, whereas Sunni law privileges paternal lineage. This fundamental divergence systematically excludes many female relatives from Sunni inheritance rights, reinforcing the patriarchal framework underpinning family law.

Within Shi'i law, inheritance follows a rigid hierarchy of entitlement, stratifying heirs by their proximity to the deceased. The primary class comprises parents, grandparents, and children; the secondary includes siblings, nieces, nephews, and grandparents; and the tertiary contains aunts, uncles, and cousins from both sides of the family. Crucially, presence of any 'first-class' heirs negates claims from lower classes, a mechanism that intensifies exclusion of more distant relatives (Ferdows, 1985: 24; Naqvi, 1968c: 362).

The Iranian Civil Code codifies these principles explicitly in Sections 861–892, where inheritance depends on 'consanguinity and special connection' (Naqvi, 1968c: 362). Notably, any form of homicide disqualifies the perpetrator from inheritance, save exceptions for self-defence, lack of intent, or legal decree (Sections 880–881, Naqvi, 1968c: 365).

Spousal inheritance occupies a distinct category, limited to permanent marriages without legal impediments (Section 940, Naqvi, 1968c: 375). The shares assigned unambiguously reveal gendered imbalance: a surviving husband receives half the estate if childless or a quarter if children exist; by contrast, a surviving wife inherits one-quarter or one-eighth respectively (Section 913, Naqvi, 1968c: 370). Egypt's 1929 draft law further underscores gender disparities, notably omitting any explicit recognition of a wife's right to inherit if the husband is presumed dead and he has surviving heirs, while actively revoking divorced wives' claims if divorce occurred over a year before his death (Articles 17 and 22, The Egyptian Gazette, 12 March 1929: 4).

Iranian law's halving of women's inheritance reflects and perpetuates their legally constructed inferiority, reinforcing the patriarchal family hierarchy. In cases of multiple surviving wives, the inheritance share allotted to a single wife is divided equally among them, with mutual inheritance rights limited to specific circumstances such as *rāj'ah* divorce during the wife's *al-'Iddah* (Sections 942–945, Naqvi, 1968c: 375–376). Complex conditions govern inheritance when illness and divorce coincide, privileging men's rights while constraining women's, with no inheritance had he been sick when they married, and subsequently died from the same illness (Sections 944–945, Naqvi, 1968c: 375–376).

Further gender disparity manifests as husbands inherit all their deceased wife's property, while wives receive only movable property and the assessed value—not the physical possession—of buildings and trees (Sections 946–947, Naqvi, 1968c: 376). Should other heirs resist paying the wife's portion, she retains the right to reclaim it directly from such assets (Section 948).

These legal provisions resonate with Qur'anic injunctions (*Sūrah* 4:11 and 4:176, Ali, 2000: 61, 80), which institutionalise men's inheritance shares at double those of women and prioritise heirs over the widowed mother, thus embedding male supremacy within religious and legal norms. This persistent religious dominance in family law stands in contrast to reformist calls for gender equality and secular governance, revealing *Reza Šah* approach of disengaging religion from the state apparatus while maintaining its pervasive role in shaping family law and societal identity.

Ultimately, the patriarchal contours of Egyptian and Iranian inheritance laws crystallise through the continued legal entrenchment of religious principles. Defenders of gendered inheritance often invoke the husband's financial obligations—such as mahr and marital support—and exemptions from military service to justify his larger share. These rationales align broadly across Sunni and Shi'i traditions (Ferdows, 1985: 25). Furthermore, in cases where the deceased is non-Muslim, Iranian law defers to the deceased's religious customs without challenge (Naqvi, 1968a: 162), signalling the complex intersections of religion, law, and gendered power in inheritance practices.

Child Custody

Child custody within *Sharī'ah* law reveals the entrenched patriarchal control extending beyond marriage into guardianship and upbringing. While mothers may retain custody in early childhood, the father—or his nearest male kin—holds guardianship rights, controlling education and the ability to contract marriages for children without maternal consent (Coulson & Hinchcliffe, 1978: 45). This legal framework operates on the premise that children 'belong' to the paternal lineage, reflecting deeply embedded notions of gender segregation, male dominance, and ownership (Harik & Marston, 1996: 99). Maternal custody is not an unconditional right, rather it is contingent upon the mother's mental, physical, and moral capacity to care for her child and her marital status, with remarriage resulting in immediate loss of custodial rights regardless of the degree of familial separation (Coulson & Hinchcliffe, 1978: 45).

The duration of maternal custody varies across Islamic jurisprudential schools, revealing divergent but uniformly patriarchal principles. *Šiʿeh-yi Ithnā ʿAshari* law restricts maternal custody of sons to two years and daughters to seven; Hanafī law extends this to seven and nine years respectively. Shafi'i law introduces child agency at age seven, allowing children to choose their custodian, while Hanbali law grants fathers automatic custody of daughters at seven, allowing boys to decide. Maliki law stands out as the most permissive, allowing mothers to retain custody until puberty for sons and including marriage as a threshold for daughters (Coulson & Hinchcliffe, 1978: 45). Yet, across these variations, the underlying patriarchal logic remains evident; fathers' rights supersede mothers', and paternal custody begins once children are deemed no longer dependent on maternal nourishment or care.

In the Egyptian legal context, child custody reflects the continuation of these religious norms, formalised within Personal Status Laws and chapter seven of the draft law of 1929. Article 20 (The Egyptian Gazette, 12th March 1929: 4) enshrines Hanafī principles, but permits judicial discretion—via the *qāḍī*—to extend maternal custody if 'in the interest of the child', allowing boys to remain with mothers until nine, and girls until eleven. However, a mother's remarriage irrevocably terminates her custodial rights, reverting children to paternal custody, which remains unchallengeable (Sadiqi & Ennaji, 2011: 136). This judicial mediation underscores the institutional dependence of women on male authority to determine their parental rights.

The 1929 reforms responded explicitly to women's complaints regarding premature custodial transfers, illustrating the negotiation between entrenched religious prescriptions and social pressures (Kholoussy, 2010: 121). Nationalist discourses, invoking maternal metaphors as the cornerstone of societal reproduction (Baron, 2005), provided ideological cover for these limited concessions, effectively functioning as a 'loophole' within immutable Islamic law that continued to privilege paternal custody in court practice (Kholoussy, 2010: 121).

Iranian family law similarly embeds *Ši'eh-yi Ithnā 'Ashari* (شیعه‌ی اثنا عشری; Twelver Shi'ism) custody principles within its Civil Code (Sections 1168–1170) and the Marriage Act (Sections 15–16), outlining the conditions for maternal custody (Naqvi, 1968a: 160; 1968b: 285). However, legal silence on the possibility of women regaining custody if fathers become unfit—physically, mentally, or morally—reflects an absence of safeguards for mothers. Moreover, no restrictions are placed on fathers remarrying, with documented cases, such as that of Taj, revealing forced separation from children as they are removed to live with their father's subsequent wife (Bamdad, 1977: 33; Amanat in al-Sultana/Vanzan & Neshati, 2003: 73). These dynamics illustrate the rigidity of custodial law and the absence of legal protections against patriarchal displacement.

Although feminists have sought reform towards gender equality and secularisation in family law, child custody remains firmly anchored in religious doctrine. The brevity of maternal custody underscores its provisional status within a patriarchal family structure. The Egyptian legal framework, despite its roots in religious law, exhibits comparatively greater flexibility by recognising the child's best interests in extending maternal custody, signalling a nuanced yet limited deviation from the rigidities observed in Iranian law.

Equality in Dissolution

Divorce laws in Egypt and Iran exemplify the entrenchment of patriarchal norms within legal structures, particularly where Islamic jurisprudence dominates family law. The disparity between male and female access to divorce is not merely legalistic; it reflects broader gendered power dynamics. Men's unilateral right to *ṭalāq* without cause contrasts starkly with the procedural hurdles women must overcome—ranging from substantiating claims of abuse or neglect to navigating the courts' often sceptical reception of their grievances. This asymmetry highlights how legal discourse codifies women's subordinate status, structurally embedding their dependency within both familial and state institutions.

Iranian legal reforms, for example, nominally permitted women to seek divorce under specific conditions such as mental illness, prolonged absence, or polygamy. However, in practice, these provisions were rarely accessible. The case of a husband obtaining divorce on health grounds with minimal resistance, while his wife faced significant evidentiary demands, underscores the gendered double standards inherent in legal interpretations. This gap between statutory language and judicial application reveals how laws, even when outwardly progressive, can remain patriarchal in effect due to interpretive bias and societal norms.

Public discourse and activism in the early twentieth century—manifested in feminist publications, demonstrations, and political lobbying—challenged these inequities. Yet these calls for reform frequently encountered resistance, especially from conservative religious authorities who positioned themselves as guardians of social morality. The endurance of patriarchal divorce laws, even amidst broader legal reforms, illustrates how religious authority was strategically maintained to regulate gender relations and uphold a specific vision of family order. Despite the broader reach of secular approaches in the public sphere, the persistence of *Sharīʿah* as the primary framework for family law reveals the enduring grip of male authority. Reforms in this domain have rarely originated from the state itself; instead, they have typically followed sustained pressure from women's rights groups, suggesting that secularism's imprint on family law remains marginal and reactive rather than transformative.

The lived experiences of women such as Huda, Doria, Taj, and Sattareh serve as empirical anchors for understanding the human impact of these legal regimes. Taj's loss of custody, where her children were transferred to their father's new wife, demonstrates how legal interpretations around maternal suitability operated less as objective assessments and more as instruments of paternal control. These narratives illuminate the emotional and social costs imposed on women by legal systems that prioritise male guardianship and uphold the sanctity of paternal lineage.

The divergent political trajectories of Egypt and Iran further complicate the relationship between secularism and gender equality. Egyptian responses to colonial encounters reveal religious resistance through state identity, with the family positioned as a key site for expressing this. As a result, *external* secularism found space primarily within the political domain, where colonial influence was most pronounced, while the private remained a stronghold of religious continuity. Meanwhile, Iran's *internal* secularisation under *Reza Šah* sought to curtail clerical influence in public life, yet notably preserved Islamic principles within family law. This selective secularisation—promoting modernisation in appearance while maintaining religious structures in substance—exposed the limits of state-driven reform in advancing women's rights.

Ultimately, family law became a contested site where competing ideologies—religious conservatism, feminist advocacy, and state nationalism—intersected. Legal reforms were shaped less by a commitment to gender equity than by the state's need to balance religious legitimacy and modern state-building. In both contexts, the persistence of gendered divorce laws underscores how women's rights remain tethered to broader political struggles over identity, authority, and the limits of secular influences.

Conclusion: Gender, Legal Reform, and the Politics of Secularism in Egypt and Iran

The complexity surrounding Islamic law and gender equality in the MENA region defies simplistic binaries often imposed by external observers. Not only do non-Western commentators contribute to the scholarly discord through their varied perspectives, but so too do Muslim adherents themselves, whose interpretations diverge across the multiple Islamic jurisprudential schools. This internal multiplicity fractures any monolithic understanding of Islamic law, revealing how debates on gender and secularism unfold simultaneously at national, communal, and individual levels. In public discourse, however, patriarchal readings of Islamic law remain entrenched, sustained by pervasive stereotypes and sweeping generalisations broadcast through diverse media channels. These narratives conflate varied religious and cultural realities into reductive East-versus-West frameworks, obscuring the nuanced ways gender equality intersects with faith and law.

A critical step lies in disentangling these Western-centric tropes from the lived experiences and reformist voices within the region, without erasing Europe's discursive imprint as what Chakrabarty (2000: 27) terms a 'sovereign, theoretical subject of all histories...'. The historiographical dominance of Europe extends even to histories claimed by Egyptians and Iranians, positioning Western modernity as the implicit benchmark against which gendered and religious identities are measured

S. Louden-Cooke, *Gender Equality, Matrimony and Secularism in Egypt and Iran: A Comparative Exploration of Early Twentieth-Century Family Law*, Middle East Today, https://doi.org/10.1007/978-3-032-00846-6_6

and contested. By shifting the analytical lens to these localised and pluralist engagements with Islamic law, this inquiry challenges the essentialising narratives that dominate both scholarly and public arenas, revealing the layered realities that shape gender justice within Islamic frameworks.

Modernity, History, and Secularism

Secularism's shape remains elusive, defying singular definition as it unfolds unevenly across states and societies. Within the Egyptian context, modernisation emerges as a crucible where a fragile national identity seeks to assert itself against a backdrop of colonial encroachment and political dependency. The imposition of British rule, alongside earlier French and Ottoman influences, fragmented Egypt's sovereignty, with settler populations not only consolidating political power but permeating social fabric. Western economic paradigms and political norms seeped into everyday life, while the adoption of Western ideals by Egyptian women—who increasingly mobilised against patriarchal oppression—signalled a profound cultural shift. This intersection of gender and nationalism unsettled established social orders, particularly as mixed marriages introduced anxieties over cultural and racial 'purity', reflecting broader fears about the erosion of indigenous identity.

Iran's experience under the *Qājār* dynasty, though not formal colonisation or protectorate status, mirrored many of Egypt's entanglements with imperial power. Political paralysis and economic instability, exacerbated by decentralised governance, allowed British and Russian forces to embed themselves within Iranian territory, with their presence felt in diverging ways across the country. The 1906 Constitutional Revolution and the 1907 Supplementary Fundamental Laws marked an ambitious era of Iranian politics. Yet, despite constitutional advocates' aspirations to curb clerical influence, religious motifs endured prominently within the political sphere, revealing the uneasy tension between tradition and modernity. Far from external influences alone, the impulse towards secular reform through the establishment of a constitution drew critical momentum from the seismic shift symbolised by Japan's victory over Tsarist Russia—an Asian constitutional power triumphing over a 'Western' non-constitutionalised autocracy—offering a blueprint for national rejuvenation divorced from imperial subjugation.

Reza Khan's ascent from the Cossack Brigade to the threshold of premiership by 1922 epitomised the drive to consolidate modern Iran through Western-inspired reforms. His cabinet, however, belied this vision; ministers like Soleiman Mirza (Eskandari), burdened by limited education and intellectual breadth, struggled to translate reformist ideals into effective policy (Ghani, 1998: 289). Nonetheless, secular transformations took tangible form through technology, the economy, and administration, with legal restructuring and the expansion of railway infrastructure being prominent (Ghani, 1998: 397). Education reforms accelerated, with compulsory schooling for children aged six to thirteen, the introduction of French curricula in secondary education, and a striking tenfold increase in female enrolment, and sixfold overall (Ghani, 1998: 399).

While Reza Khan projected an image of authority and resolve, critics within intellectual and political circles questioned the depth of his engagement with political theories. His public stance offered little indication of a coherent strategy to navigate, let alone reconcile, the entrenched religious-secular divide that characterised Iranian society (Ghani, 1998: 299). At the same time, a growing chorus of secularist writers and reformist thinkers—though wary of his limitations—converged around him as the only viable figure capable of imposing order and initiating reform. Their advocacy helped shape a state that increasingly adopted the external markers of secular modernity: Western legal codes, European-style dress, and institutional restructuring. Yet these transformations ran parallel to a persistent religious undercurrent. The result of this, and his *internally secular* approach, was a dual reality of an Iranian state which was outwardly aligned with secular modernism, yet inwardly tethered to its religious traditions.

The veneer of secularism in Iran revealed contradictions as public scepticism mounted by 1922 (TNA, FO 416/112, 1932: 11), underscoring doubts about Reza Khan's vision amid persistent social fissures. The lingering legacy of World War One exacerbated internal fragilities, with refugee flows intensifying economic and humanitarian pressures (TNA, FO 416/112, 1932: 65). Concurrently, foreign interest in Iran's natural resources, especially from the United States in the oil-rich northern provinces (TNA, FO 416/112, 1932: 19), reinforced the country's exposure to external material ambitions. In this, Iran's predicament resonated closely with Egypt's with both states bore the weight of imperialist designs while negotiating contested paths towards self-definition and secular modernity.

Women's struggles for matrimonial equality illuminated a shared bottom-up impetus for reform in both countries. In Egypt and Iran, the intertwining of education and feminist consciousness emerged as a critical fulcrum, where campaigns against illiteracy, superstition, and disease coalesced into demands for legal and social recognition. Unlike the United States' feminist movements a century earlier, which had encountered vigorous resistance to female education, Iranian advocates faced entrenched opposition that limited the scope of reform (Sanasarian, 1982: 48). Yet in both Egypt and Iran, women's writings, salons, boycotts, and marches forged visible arenas of contestation, articulating calls to restrict polygamy, regulate male divorce, and expand healthcare and educational access. Nationalist and gendered rhetoric became intertwined tools for framing women's liberation as integral to the nation's emancipation. Notably, Reza Khan's tolerance of charitable activities aligned with his constructed vision of women's social roles (Sanasarian, 1982: 68), allowing certain women's groups to operate within tightly circumscribed boundaries (Sanasarian, 1982: 68).

Examining these dynamics through the prism of political history foregrounds secularism's uneven emergence as shaped by imperial incursions and domestic political agency. In Iran, robust governmental voices pushed for secular reforms, while in Egypt, secularism was more prominently imposed or facilitated through colonial authority, creating a dichotomy between 'internal' and 'external' secularisms. This distinction illuminates how secularism was introduced in each state and thus how power was negotiated, contested, and co-opted within two culturally distinct yet historically entangled contexts.

The inquiry into matrimonial equality, therefore, reveals more than gender politics alone; it uncovers the intertwined forces of nationalism, colonialism, and modernisation that shaped Egypt and Iran during the early twentieth century. The feminist voices and political actors of this period stand as witnesses to the complex interplay of resistance and accommodation, highlighting how secularism's promises and limits were lived, contested, and reimagined. Through this comparative lens, the intricate mosaics of power, identity, and reform in Egypt and Iran emerge with renewed clarity, enriching our understanding of secularism's variegated trajectories in the modern MENA region.

Matrimonial Equality

Marriage functioned as the cornerstone of familial and social structures in both Egypt and Iran, formally integrating new individuals into society's fabric. Yet, through the testimonies and memories of key Egyptian and Iranian women, a pattern emerges whereby marriage was often experienced not as a union of affection but as transactional and orchestrated predominantly by men. Women's exclusion from the choice of partner and the negotiation of marriage contracts frankly illustrated the entrenched patriarchal authority exercised by fathers and male guardians. This exclusion, deeply rooted in custom, was frequently justified through age; daughters were married off as children, with paternal authority extending well into their adult lives.

Legal frameworks further entrenched these dynamics. Egyptian laws 25/1920, 33/1926, and 25/1929 (NWRO, n.d.), alongside the Iranian Civil Code (Taleghany, 1995) and the Marriage Act of Iran (Naqvi, 1967, 1968a, 1968b, 1968c), codified distinct and overlapping marital rights, embedding traditional and religious values within increasingly secular legislative language. Six principal marital rights claimed by men surfaced consistently across both states:

1. To marry
2. Being a *wali*
3. Choosing a partner
4. Prohibit paid work
5. Financial prerogatives
6. Multiple wives

First is the right to marry. This is conferred not only the agency to choose a wife but also to act as *wali*, thus arranging marriages for others, predominantly daughters. This links to the second right, which is that of guardianship in relation to paternal roles in marrying off daughters, or an appointed role to find a suitor; accompanied with the right to choose partners, this reaffirms male dominance within familial hierarchies. Men further exercised control by influencing work restrictions on non-domestic women and by having financial prerogatives in setting mahr and maintenance, thereby curbing potential financial claims from brides or their families. Polygamy, permitted under both legal systems, symbolised and institutionalised male privilege, contingent on the husband's ability to maintain equitable treatment of multiple wives.

Restrictive measures circumscribed both sexes, though the locus of control often remained male. Again, six were identified, with two being shared and four only applicable in Iran:

1. Male agency removed if married as a child (shared)
2. Consent from *wali* (shared)
3. Stipulations prohibited if linked to ending marriage
4. Deception was a criminal offence
5. Government approval for mixed marriages
6. Puberty was the (initial) benchmark for female marriage

Boys married as children lost agency in choosing partners, equating their position with that of girls and women, reinforcing parental dominion. Consent from a woman's guardian remained a gatekeeping mechanism, effectively preventing unions absent of male approval. Iranian law imposed further constraints on both men and women, with stipulations threatening contract revocation not being permitted. Furthermore, deception by either party in the establishment or completion of the marriage risked imprisonment. Later legal reforms introduced state oversight of mixed marriages, requiring government consent, reflecting anxieties over cultural and national identity. Age restrictions, particularly in Iran where puberty marked legal eligibility, attempted to regulate marriageable age but left significant interpretative latitude.

Shared marital rights between couples existed but were often framed within patriarchal legal contexts, with five of them being identified and most only within the Iranian context:

1. End an engagement (shared)
2. Return any gifts to the other person (shared)
3. Outsource marriage contracting to a third party
4. Temporary marriage
5. *Mahr* was a legal requirement in *sigheh*

Both Egypt and Iran permitted dissolution of betrothals and mandated return of gifts, yet Iranian law allowed for the delegation of contracting marriages to third parties, further marginalising direct spousal agency.

Iran's recognition of *sigheh*, absent in Egypt, demanded a formal *mahr*, highlighting divergent legal understandings of marital forms.

Gendered hierarchies permeated the legal landscape of both countries with some rights and restrictions only relating to one sex. Men's rights encompassed polygamy (up to four wives), partner selection barring childhood, or child, marriages—with the vague benchmark of 'puberty' being used as guidance, and freedom to marry outside the Muslim faith or nationality (more permissible for men than women). Iranian law explicitly safeguarded a man's right to retain his nationality in cases of mixed marriage, a provision not extended to women. While Egypt's legal texts were less explicit on this matter, Kholoussy (2003, 2010) highlights prevailing concerns about the influence of foreign husbands—suggesting that, in practice, a similar gendered asymmetry may have been in effect. Legal privileges for men extended further: if a wife failed to perform her legally defined duties, husbands could withhold *mahr* and maintenance without legal consequence. Until 1931, this position was even more pronounced in the case of *sigheh*, where maintenance obligations existed only if they were negotiated and agreed upon before the union was formalised. Although Islamic law imposed numerical limits on polygamy in both jurisdictions, Iranian legal interpretations exempted *sigheh* from these constraints—permitting men to enter into multiple such unions without restriction.

Conversely, women in both states were able to sue for unpaid *mahr* or maintenance; later deciding how it was to be spent. Knowledge of existing and subsequent wives was required when the marriage was contracted, and the ability to stipulate conditions in marriage contracts—though such clauses only gained legal recognition in Iran, with it being adopted in Egypt as a socio-cultural tradition. The absence of mandatory health certificates for child brides suggested underlying assumptions about female purity; there is, however, no mention of this for older women. Finally, women's legal ability to refuse conjugal relations in cases of venereal disease acknowledged some bodily autonomy, while reinforcing the governments prioritisation of a healthy female body.

Four key marital rights stood out for women in both states:

1. *Mahr*
2. Maintenance
3. Minimum age
4. *To be* married

Both Egyptian and Iranian laws guaranteed mahr and maintenance, with Egyptian brides reportedly receiving between one-third and one-half of *mahr* prior to marriage. Legal minimum marriage ages emerged as significant feminist victories, affirming a (female) child's right to a childhood and protection from risks associated with bearing children at a young age; though societal enforcement remained inconsistent and problematic. Finally, and controversially, the notion of a 'woman's right to be married' emerged, reflecting the paradox that while women were positioned as central to marriage's social order, their autonomy within this institution was heavily circumscribed.

This detailed examination reveals that Egypt's most tangible feminist success was securing legal minimum marriage ages, though entrenched social and economic pressures undercut its effectiveness. Iran's analogous provisions, while nominally protective, remained vague and insufficient in practice. Naqvi's critique (1967: 241) that Iranian laws lacked substantive impact mirrors similar assessments of Egyptian statutes. Across both states, material rights—financial maintenance and contractual participation—constituted the bulk of women's legal entitlements, while substantive marital autonomy and equality remained elusive.

Equality in the Dissolution of a Marriage

The termination of marriage unfolds through two principal avenues: divorce, as an active decision dissolving the marital contract, and the passive dissolution precipitated by the death of a spouse. Close examination of Egyptian and Iranian legal codes reveals a consistent theme—the endurance of male dominance within both processes, despite reforms ostensibly aimed at expanding women's rights.

Within the realm of divorce, four dominant male privileges emerge:

1. Ease of divorce
2. No evidence or judge required
3. Refund on additional *mahr* if marriage was not consummated (Iran)
4. Unconditional child custody (Iran, but varied between schools)

Chief among these is the ease with which men can initiate divorce, a feature championed by feminist movements in both Egypt and Iran. This is compounded by the absence of procedural safeguards, as men are not required to present evidence or seek judicial approval. Iranian law further codifies this imbalance by entitling men to reclaim any additional portion of the *mahr* paid in advance, which exceeded half the total amount, should divorce occur prior to consummation, effectively quantifying the dissolution as a financial transaction. Post-divorce, paternal authority persists through unconditional child custody following the end of maternal custody, unless the mother's rights are revoked, underscoring a legal system that privileges men's control over children's lives.

Yet, restrictions exist on both sexes during dissolution, though these often reinforce existing hierarchies:

1. Paternal annulment (Egypt)
2. Repudiation restrictions
3. Conditional repudiation not permitted (Iran)
4. Knowledge of menstruation invalidated divorce (Iran)
5. *Rāj'ah* divorce banned for wives younger than 9 years old (Iran)
6. Divorce not permitted on the grounds of a known, pre-existing health blemish (Iran)

Egyptian law, for instance, empowers a woman's father to annul her marriage should he produce evidence of her husband's inferior social standing, sidelining both spouses' agency and underscoring class considerations as a governing principle in marital legitimacy. Other constraints focus on limiting male excesses. Repudiations executed under duress or intoxication are invalid in both countries, while Iranian law explicitly prohibits conditional repudiation used as a tool of spousal control; forbidding *rāj'ah* divorce if the wife was under nine years old. Moreover, divorce during menstruation was invalid unless exceptional circumstances applied, such as absence and thus a lack of awareness. Crucially, Iranian law bars divorce on the grounds of a 'health blemish' existing at the time of marriage, thereby absolving husbands from culpability for harm inflicted post-marriage, a provision effectively shielding male spouses from criminal liability.

Legal provisions granted for both men and women, predominantly in Iran, include:

1. The right to initiate divorce
2. Divorce because of deception in stipulations (Iran)
3. Divorce because of insanity (Iran)
4. Divorce because of blemishes outlined in law (Iran)
5. Inherit from each other (Iran)

In both Egypt and Iran, men and women were given the right to initiate divorce. Iranian statutes permit dissolution in cases of contractual deceit or proven insanity, irrespective of permanence, with legally prescribed criteria shaping permissibility for divorce based on poor health (Naqvi, 1968b: 358; Taleghany, 1995: 163–164). Both spouses may also inherit from one another absent legal impediments, indicating some degree of reciprocal rights post-marriage.

However, male privileges persist distinctively, with men also being able to:

1. Reconcile during *al-ʿIddah*
2. Stop maintenance after *al-ʿIddah* (Iran)
3. Reclaim *mahr* (Iran)
4. Relinquish remaining time in a temporary marriage (Iran)

In *rājʿah* divorces, men retain the prerogative to reconcile during *al-ʿIddah*, with Iranian law further allowing husbands to cease maintenance after *al-ʿIddah* in the case of *ṭalāqun bā'inun* and to reclaim *mahr* if divorce follows consummation for reasons other than impotency. *Sigheh* also reflect male prerogatives, and husbands may terminate contracts prematurely, relinquishing wives before the agreed term.

Women's rights in dissolution, while legally acknowledged, remained circumscribed in both states:

1. Sue for unpaid finances
2. Apply for divorce if mistreated
3. Maintenance until *al-ʿIddah*/pregnancy ended (Egypt)
4. Maintenance beyond *al-ʿIddah*/pregnancy if *rājʿah* (Iran)
5. *Mahr al-Mithl* for unknowingly consummating an invalid marriage (Iran)
6. *Sigheh*—retain *mahr* in death (Iran)
7. *Sigheh*—half *mahr* if ended early and not consummated (Iran)
8. Request extension to maternal custody (Egypt)

They may sue for unpaid mahr and maintenance, and petition courts for divorce on grounds of maltreatment. In addition to being able to request divorce, maintenance continued until the end of *al-ʿIddah* or pregnancy, with Iranian law extending support beyond these periods in *rājʿah* divorces. Unique to Iranian law, women unaware of marriage invalidity upon consummation could receive *Mahr al-Mithl*; while in *sigheh*, the wife retains mahr regardless of consummation, her death, or premature contract termination. Unlike Iran, Egyptian law also permits women to seek extended child custody if deemed in the child's best interests, suggesting marginal recognition of maternal agency.

In addition to this, five further rights specific to women were evidenced:

1. Termination of pre-pubescent marriages (Egypt)
2. Entitled to full amount of remaining *mahr*, lowering to half if not consummated (Egypt)
3. Entitled to full amount of remaining *mahr* if no total was agreed/mentioned prior to consummation (Iran)
4. Entitled to full amount of remaining *mahr* if there was ambiguity over form/ownership abilities (Iran)
5. Request divorce for poor financial support or incurable illness (Iran)

Egyptian law allowed termination upon reaching puberty if marriage occurred prior to this. Both Egyptian and Iranian laws guarantee the full payment of outstanding *mahr* if the marriage had been consummated, dropping to half if it had not been. Full entitlement was also outlined in cases where the contract lacked amount specificities prior to consummation. In addition to mistreatment, women could seek divorce if husbands failed to financially support her, or were incurably ill. Iranian law also safeguarded full mahr entitlements where ambiguity or ownership barriers existed. Yet, applications for divorce demanded evidence, reinforcing barriers to women's autonomous marital exit.

Inheritance rights and restrictions reveal further gender disparities:

- Silence regarding presumption of husband's death (Egypt)
- No inheritance if divorced for over 1 year and dispute arises (Egypt)
- Inherit a percentage of husband's estate (Iran)
- Equally divided among multiple wives (Iran)

Egyptian law remained silent on wives' entitlement when husbands are presumed dead after prolonged absence (*The Egyptian Gazette*, 1929: 4), and excludes divorced women's inheritance after a year of separation and a dispute arose. Conversely, Iranian law permits women to inherit proportional shares of their husband's estate, with multiple wives dividing the allocated share equally.

Between the two modes of marital dissolution, death represents a more constrained arena for gender equality. Yet divorce, though seemingly offering more legal avenues for women, remains heavily skewed towards male prerogatives. Women's advocates in Egypt and Iran fixated on the disproportionate ease with which men secured divorce, highlighting this as a core site of patriarchal power. Although legal stipulations circumscribing divorce validity, discouraging *rājʿah* divorces, and permitting conditional female-initiated divorce might suggest progress, these measures largely function to reaffirm entrenched gender hierarchies and women's marginalised status within both legal and social domains.

Women, Secularism, and the State

The politicisation of the private sphere manifests in multiple dimensions—beginning with the classical public/private dichotomy and extending to the state's increasing intervention into private life. However, it is not only the private sphere that became politicised, but also the bodies and identities of those within it. Through legal regulation of marriage—including who may marry, the roles and responsibilities of spouses, and the conditions under which a marriage may be dissolved—this book argues that the private sphere was effectively transformed into a secondary site of political governance. While ostensibly remaining under the purview of religious authority, the private sphere's legal entanglement with state structures meant its boundaries increasingly blurred with those of the secular, public domain. In this way, personal and familial life was not merely regulated but subsumed into the wider political project of social ordering.

In the decades preceding the mid-twentieth century, Egypt and Iran witnessed a burgeoning feminist awareness, its roots embedded in the dissonance between public aspirations and private constraints. Women such as Huda Shaarawi and Taj al-Saltana did not merely document oppression; they embodied it. The cloistered anguish of child marriage, the premature assumption of maternal responsibilities, and the stifling boundaries of conjugal obedience wove themselves into narratives that catalysed collective consciousness. Taj, reflective in her memoirs (al-Sultana/Vanzan & Neshati, n.d./2003: 201), cast her gaze towards Europe, imagining emancipated women not only as distant kin but as potential futures for Iranian women. This yearning did not emerge from ignorance of Western complexities but from a sharpened awareness of local inequities.

By examining the perspectives of external actors and the sharpened scrutiny applied to women's rights, it becomes possible to trace the indirect effects of secularism on matrimonial equality in the women's movements of Egypt and Iran. While Western models of gender reform and secular governance offered points of reference and inspiration, they were not the sole catalysts for local activism. This book contends that the impetus for change was rooted primarily in the lived experiences of women within these societies. Their growing awareness of the entrenched legal and cultural inequalities in matrimonial relations—combined with a desire to protect future generations from similar injustices—was instrumental in galvanising reformist efforts. Thus, rather than being passively shaped by external ideals, the movements were driven by a conscious, internal push to redress gender imbalances within marriage through locally grounded struggles and prevent future generations from having similar experiences.

This dynamic is particularly evident with Huda Sha'arawi (1987; Sharawi Lanfranchi, 2012) and Taj al-Saltaneh (n.d./2003), both of whom endured child marriage, early motherhood, and the gendered restrictions imposed during married life. However, it is important to note a key distinction in the nature of their respective marriages. While Huda was married to a man significantly older than herself, Taj's husband was still a child at the time of their union. Despite these differing marital configurations, both women's experiences contributed to a broader feminist awakening, both personally and collectively. Their narratives, rooted in the intimate domain of marriage, serve as powerful illustrations of how the private sphere became internally politicised. In this context, personal adversity became a catalyst for political consciousness, revealing the ways in which private suffering could be transformed into public resistance and feminist critique.

Early twentieth-century Egypt and Iran experienced distinct yet intertwined secularising processes that significantly influenced national and gender discourses. In Egypt, the 1919 revolution and the subsequent granting of semi-independence in 1922 marked a pivotal nationalist moment in which women's rights gained unprecedented public prominence (Al-Ali, 2000). These emerging feminist discourses did not merely align with nationalist rhetoric; they also interrogated its limitations and exclusions. Within both Egypt and Iran, the socio-political upheavals of this era ignited a broader demand for self-definition. Central to these struggles were contested notions of authenticity and identity, which became foundational to reconfigurations of both national and gender politics (Al-Ali, 2000). In this context, feminist activism was not simply a byproduct of nationalism, but a dynamic force shaping and challenging the very meaning of modernity and independence in both societies.

Huda Shaarawi's activism, including her success in securing women's access to university education and establishing a minimum marriage age (Talhami, 1996: 12), did not merely punctuate Egyptian feminist history, it symbolised a strategic penetration into legal structures. In Egypt, the discourse on unveiling, visibly embodied in Huda's and Safiyya Zaghloul's 1924 unveiling, differed markedly from Iranian priorities. For Egyptians, the veil signified a barricade between women and public engagement (Talhami, 1996: 13); for Iranians, as Sanasarian (1982: 65–66) notes, other urgencies overshadowed its symbolism. This contrast reflects the divergent secular configurations of the two states. Moaddel and Azadarmaki (2002) elucidate the paradox noting that public religiosity and the state's identity do not often correlate. The veil thus operated as a complex symbol of resistance, shaped not only by patriarchy but by the religio-political topography of each nation, with an externally secular state prioritising other issues over those of female appearance, while not overlooking the complexities of the veil completely, and an internally secular state attempting to quell symbolic components of religious and patriarchal oppression.

Beneath this surface, the women's organisations diverged in their aspirations. Iran's National Ladies Society (1910), focused on national sovereignty, often externalised the blame for women's conditions, attributing their plight to foreign interference (Sanasarian, 1985: 94). Conversely, the later Jamiet Nesvan Vatankhah Iran (1922), aligned more closely with the ethos of *Al-Ittihād Al-Nisā'ī Al-Miṣrī*, targeting internal societal reform through education and opposition to child marriage. Neither movement sought to undermine Islam outright; rather, both critiqued patriarchal misinterpretations of its tenets. Islamic fidelity coexisted with gender advocacy, a dual commitment visible in both Iranian and Egyptian feminist circles (Sanasarian, 1985: 97).

Within this milieu, secularism did not offer liberation in any absolute sense. Reforms throughout the early twentieth century, though framed as feminist victories, often served to entrench state control and patriarchal norms. What appeared as advancement, such as legal age mandates and expanded divorce provisions, frequently operated as mechanisms of containment. Instead of disrupting religious authority over the private sphere, secularism rearticulated its terms. Thus, legal texts and policies camouflaged enduring inequalities, legitimising them under the guise of reform.

The public secularisation of Egypt and Iran, driven by colonising forces and domestic modernisers like Reza Khan, was met with grassroots responses aiming to redefine societal norms. Feminist and nationalist groups invoked secular idioms, not to mimic Western paradigms, but to challenge theocratic rigidity and colonial imposition alike. In this context, secularism became a terrain of contestation: for the state, a tool of governance; for gender equality activists, a potential, but deeply compromised, path to female autonomy.

Secularisation can thus be understood as embedded within state-society relations in Egypt and Iran through the implementation of increasingly secular policies, the rise of women's literature, and sustained encounters with Western ideologies and colonial presence. In this context, secularism influenced women's marital rights by offering a conceptual and institutional framework through which power, both state and individual, emerged. This power manifested in two distinct ways: first, as the authority of the state over its citizens; and second, as the personal autonomy of citizens, particularly women, in navigating private life. It was within this evolving framework that women became increasingly aware of the dangers of child marriage, the significance of partner choice, and the gendered imbalance in divorce laws.

Despite the persistence of religious law in family matters, secularism did not entirely displace Islam but often worked in tandem with it. Traditional values remained influential, yet Islam was also increasingly presented as compatible with women's rights and autonomy. Across both states, secularism was closely associated with modernisation, even as its reach into the private sphere remained contested and incomplete.

In Egypt, perhaps the most tangible legal gain was the establishment of a minimum age for marriage for both sexes. In contrast, Iran's legal system employed the more ambiguous criterion of puberty, offering limited protection. However, Iranian women were able to include specific stipulations in marriage contracts—provided they did not pertain to divorce—which offered some potential for greater marital security. While both legal systems theoretically allowed women to seek divorce, the right to initiate it remained predominantly in male hands. The Iranian Civil Code and Marriage Act, as well as Egyptian legal reforms, largely reinforced a framework of female dependence on male authority.

Although Iran appeared to make more numerous reforms concerning divorce, these changes were often superficial. Women were required to obtain permission from male authorities, rendering legal autonomy largely symbolic. Thus, both Egypt and Iran ultimately maintained patriarchal structures within family law, and reforms remained minimal and tightly constrained. Crucially, this persistence of inequality cannot be attributed solely to the influence of *Sharīʿah* law. Rather, it was the continued use of patriarchal interpretations of *Sharīʿah* that prevented the transformative potential of secularism—so visible in other political and legal spheres—from extending into the private domain.

Taj al-Saltaneh's memoirs, though limited in scope, reveal a personal account emblematic of broader societal tensions. As Amanat notes (in al-Sultana/Vanzan & Neshati, n.d./2003: 9), she stands as a symbol 'of the emerging secular intelligentsia' and as a feminist voice articulating the complexities of a society in transition. Her narrative reinforces the argument that while secularism left a discernible imprint on women's movements, it did not necessarily transform the legal status of women within the family.

Ultimately, while Egypt and Iran share regional and colonial histories, their approaches to matrimonial equality during this period reveal a parallel trajectory of minimal legal reform, limited feminist gains in the private sphere, and continued subjugation of women under a hybrid legal framework that privileged patriarchal interpretations of religion, even as secularism gained influence in other domains.

This duality surfaced acutely in more contemporary marital law. In Egypt, Law 25/1925 and its subsequent amendments (1979, 1985, 2000, 2004) illustrate a back-and-forth struggle. In 1971, constitutional deliberations in Egypt raised the issue of incorporating *Sharīʿah* as a principal source of legislation, prompting renewed attention to family law reform. By 1979, amendments to the Personal Status Laws marked a significant development, and women were granted the right to seek divorce on the grounds of polygamy, provided they filed within a twelve-month period of the subsequent marriage.

However, in 1985, these reforms were reversed on procedural grounds, as the People's Assembly had not been in session when the amendments were enacted. The annulment of these laws revoked women's automatic right to divorce in cases of polygamy. Although women retained the ability to appeal for divorce, their claims had to demonstrate harm to the family in order to be approved by a *qāḍī*. In cases where divorce was granted, the *qāḍī* was also responsible for designating appropriate housing for the wife and children, further institutionalising judicial control over women's post-divorce circumstances.

Concurrently, twelve stipulations were introduced into the Iranian marriage contract, allowing women the right to initiate divorce—conditional, however, on the husband's prior agreement to each clause (Keddie, 2001). Although these provisions were not as comprehensive as those previously enshrined in the Family Protection Law of 1967, several elements of the annulled law were partially reinstated after the 1979 Islamic Revolution. Among these were the establishment of special family courts to adjudicate domestic disputes and, later, issues of child custody. Additionally, women were entitled to claim up to half of the property acquired during marriage, provided they had not consented to the divorce (Keddie, 2001).

Despite resistance from conservatives to maternal custody, irrespective of remarriage, the Iranian legislature enacted a 1985 bill that authorised limited state financial assistance to divorced women for the 'upkeep of needs' (Keddie, 2001). In a further effort to regulate marital dissolution, a 1989 law introduced the requirement that court approval be obtained before a divorce could be officially registered. While adherence to *Sharīʿah* law became more pronounced following the formation of the Islamic Republic of Iran, demographic data suggests a gradual decline in traditional child marriage. By 1986, the average age of marriage for women had risen to twenty, increasing further to twenty-two by 1996 (Keddie, 2001).

In early 2000s Egypt, a woman seeking to escape an unhappy marriage could finally do so through *khulʿ* divorce, so long as she gave up her financial rights. This legal recognition, encoded in Article 20 of Law 1/2000, offered a narrow window of autonomy, but only at a cost that reinforced economic dependence on men. In Iran, 2007 saw the introduction of a Family Protection Bill. Public backlash to its most discriminatory provisions followed swiftly in 2008, led by the One Million Signatures campaign (FIS, n.d.).

By 2008, Egypt had legally raised the marriage age to eighteen; yet, this protection was later destabilised under new constitutional reforms (ECWR, 2012). Three years later, the UN reported that Egypt had no laws against marital rape or sexual harassment, but did have one against domestic violence; leaving countless women without recourse. In Iran, even basic legal data remained unavailable, hiding women's realities behind bureaucratic opacity (*The Guardian*, 2011).

The state's priorities became clearer in Iran's *Bill 315*, which urged women to marry young, bear more children, and avoid divorce; all in the name of 'family exaltation'. Critics warned that this bill did not just fail to protect women; it endangered them (Amnesty International, 2015: 6). Meanwhile, the Iranian Civil Code continued to define a woman's life by permission: permission to work outside the home, permission to retain custody, permission to divorce—conditions rarely mirrored in law for men. Even *sigheh*, legally sanctioned, left women vulnerable to abandonment under the guise of legality (FIS, n.d.). Bill 315 also

> entrusts multiple state bodies with developing and promoting "an Islamic-Iranian life style" rooted in "traditional" family values and gender-role stereotypes that present women's primary role as wives and mothers, based on "guidelines" of the Supreme Leader. (Amnesty International, 2015: 7)

In 2012, Supreme Leader Ayatollah Ali Khamenei publicly condemned Iran's social policies for imitating Western lifestyles, reinforcing the ideological critique of *gharbzadegī* and signalling a renewed commitment to Islamic orthodoxy, particularly in the regulation of gender relations (Amnesty International, 2015: 7). This pronouncement was not merely rhetorical but was followed by concrete shifts in the legal apparatus governing the private sphere. Concurrently, Egypt was undergoing the volatile aftermath of the 2011 uprisings. The brief tenure of the Muslim Brotherhood was marked by heightened public anxieties around gender norms, particularly following widespread reports of sexual violence targeting both Egyptian and foreign women.

Although it is not possible to assert a direct causal relationship between Egypt's revolutionary moment and the subsequent hardening of Iranian legal structures, the temporal proximity of these developments invites critical scrutiny. The Iranian state's intensification of gendered legal constraints during this period may be read as part of a broader defensive strategy to preserve ideological boundaries perceived to be under threat. Thus, the legal containment of women's autonomy functioned not only as an assertion of religious fidelity but also as a mechanism for insulating the state from the perceived destabilising effects of regional socio-political transformation.

Meanwhile, *'irfiyy* marriages gained traction in Egypt, driven by religious prominence, economic precarity and reinforced by legal ambiguity. This not only counters regulations regarding pre-marital sex, but it has become increasingly popular due to 'The costs of a regular marriage and the obligations that go with it…' (Knell, 2010). Concerns regarding female security in such marriages have arisen. While *'irfiyy* marriages have been legally recognised in Egypt since 2000, women have struggled to prove paternity of children as was evidenced by the controversy surrounding actors Zeina and Ezz (Lambert & Ramadan, 2015), and Hind al-Hinnawy and Ahmad al-Fishawy (Hasso, 2011). In Iran, *sigheh*, legally sanctioned yet socially fraught, mirror similar dynamics.

Since then, the intensification of veiling laws in Iran has been 'promoted' as further protecting the sanctity of the family, with the lived reality being far more oppressive for Iranian women. The 'Law on Protecting the Family through the Promotion of the Culture of Chastity and Hijab' came into force on 13 December 2024, with the female population facing up to 15 years imprisonment, or the death penalty, for failing to wear a hijab (correctly) in 'physical and online spaces', with experts describing it as 'an intensification of State control over women's bodies in Iran and a further assault on women's rights and freedoms' (UN, 2024). However, on December 14th, the Supreme National Security Council, broke precedent and intervened to halt this bill (Kahalzadeh, 2024), which received intense criticism from within and outside of the state.

In 2022, Egyptian President Adbel Fattah El-Sisi proposed a Family Support Fund which was designed to support more vulnerable, divorced women whose husbands had defaulted on alimony payments, with fees being 'paid by marrying couples'; with rumours of US$723 (20,000 Egyptian pounds) being denied (LOC, 2023). In addition to this, financial situations for divorced women could thus be treated as an 'urgent legal matter'; with Law 6/2020 sentencing a man who defaults for 3 months to up to 12 months imprisonment, a fine, or both (LOC, 2023). It was also proposed that marrying couples 'would be required to undergo medical and psychological tests', with results being submitted to a family law judge who could then (not) allow a *ma'zoun* (marriage officiator) to formalise the marriage (LOC, 2023), thus reflecting earlier Iranian health practices.

Further amendments were then finalised at the start of 2025, seeking to equalise and modernise aspects of Egyptian family law, with specific references to divorce and child custody; requiring men to register verbal divorces within 15 days, prioritising maternal custody, with paternal custody moving from 16th to 2nd option (Egyptian Streets, 2025).

The historical records of Egypt and Iran, which have shaped the trajectories each state has taken to reach the contemporary realities outlined above, reveal a complex interplay: increased secularisation of the public sphere resulted in family law becoming further entrenched in religious law. Consequently, this legalistic retreat indicates a protective mechanism for the private sphere, thus ensuring the continuation of Islamic traditions and the maintenance of an 'authentically' Islamic identity at society's foundations.

Divergent secular trajectories in Egypt and Iran played a critical role in shaping the scope and nature of women's marital rights. In Egypt, the legacy of direct British occupation and its formal status as a Protectorate after 1914 left enduring imprints on the structure of governance and the ideological framing of secularism. While colonial administrations often professed a reluctance to intervene in domains governed by religious law—particularly family law (Asad, 2003: 227)—the imposition of secularised reforms in industrial spheres produced unintended spillover effects. These reforms reconfigured economic relations within Egyptian society, indirectly exerting pressure on the private sphere through issues such as the rise in *mahr* demands during this period.

In Iran, where British involvement was more economically strategic than territorially dominant, similar patterns emerged. Despite the absence of formal colonial governance, imperial entanglements—particularly in the realms of oil, infrastructure, and trade—stimulated state-led modernisation efforts that mirrored colonial logics. These included secular reforms in education and legal rationalisation, which, while ostensibly leaving family law untouched, created new economic conditions that reverberated through domestic arrangements.

Taken together, these cases illustrate how imperial power, whether exercised through direct rule or indirect influence, operated as a structural force that redefined gendered rights and responsibilities within marriage. The secularisation of the public sphere, particularly in its economic dimension, subtly but materially reshaped the contours of the private sphere, demonstrating that colonial power could recalibrate marital norms without directly legislating upon them.

Throughout the twentieth century, the secular character of both Egypt and Iran proved to be fluid, contingent upon shifts in political leadership and the prevailing interpretations of religious identity. In the early twentieth century, secularism, though variably articulated in each context, played a formative role in shaping the trajectory of women's marital rights. In Egypt, the separation of religion from politics facilitated the emergence of women's rights discourses within a nationalist framework, while in Iran, secularism manifested more as the withdrawal of religion from the (public), rather than from politics per se. These divergent models of secularism influenced the evolution of both religious and non-religious gender women's rights movements and provoked distinct policy responses that continue to shape gender relations today.

The persistence of patriarchal interpretations of religious law suggests that advocacy for women's rights in both contexts will continue to operate within a hybrid terrain—negotiating both religious and secular discourses. While these interpretations often function to circumscribe women's autonomy, their implications are not uniform. In Iran, for instance, policies such as Bill 315 exemplify the state's continued politicisation of women's bodies by codifying their reproductive and familial roles. In contrast, in Egypt, practices such as *ʿirfīyy* marriages expose women to legal and economic vulnerabilities, reinforcing informal patriarchal structures even in the absence of state sanction.

The historical oscillation between religious and secular authority in both states complicates efforts to forecast the future of women's rights. This unpredictability stems from the inherently subjective and context-dependent nature of religion, secularism, and lived experience. In this regard, Kedourie's (1993: 138–139) reflections on the erratic spread and impact of nationalism may be extended to the evolving interplay between secularism, gender equality, and state ideologies. Just as nationalism has defied linear trajectories across different contexts, so too do the futures of secular and religious gender politics resist definitive projection.

Glossary of Persian Terms

Society (organisation)	*Anjuman*	انجمن
The Society of Women's Efforts	*Anjuman-i Himmat-i Khavatin*	انجمن همت خواتين
The Society of Iran's Women	*Anjuman-i Khvātīn-i Iran*	انجمن خواتين ايران
The Society of Ladies of the Homeland	*Anjuman-i Mukhaddarāt-i Vatan*	انجمن مخدرات وطن
The Society of Women	*Anjuman-i Nisvān*	انجمن نسوان
Knowledge	*Dāneš*	دانش
State	*daulat*	دولت
Religion	*dīn*	دين
Westoxication	*gharbzadegī*	غربـزدگی
The Council of Women of the Centre	*Hay'at-i Khavātīn-i Markazi*	هيئت خواتين مرکزی
National Will (Initiative)	*Erāde-yi-i Millī*	اراده ملی
Twelver Shi'ism	*Ši'eh-yi Ithnā 'Ashari*	شيعه‌ی اثنا عشری
The Secret Union of Women	*Ittihādiyah-yi makhfī-i Nisvān*	اتحاديه مخفی نسوان
The Union of Women	*Ittihādiyah-yi Nisvān*	اتحاديه نسوان
Freedom Seeking Ladies	*Zanān-i āzādī'khāh*	زنان آزادی‌خواه
Viceroy	*Nāyib al-Saltaneh*	نايب‌السلطنه
Religious council/Parliament	*Majles*	مجلس
Modern intelligentsia/ Enlightened thinkers	*Munavver al-fekr*	منورالفکر
Milk price	*Šir baha*	بها شير

S. Louden-Cooke, *Gender Equality, Matrimony and Secularism in Egypt and Iran: A Comparative Exploration of Early Twentieth-Century Family Law*, Middle East Today, https://doi.org/10.1007/978-3-032-00846-6

Women's Voice	*Zabān-e Zanān*	زبان زنان
A suit (suitor)	Khāstgārī (Khāstgār)	خواستگاری (خواستگار)
King	Śah	شاه
Iranian Women's Rights Movement	Jonbeś-i zanān-i iran	جنبش زنان ایران
Blossom	*Šokūfeh*	شکوفه
Morality police	*Gašt-e eršâd*	گشت ارشاد
Shari'a	*Sharīʿat*	شریعت
Dowry	*mahriyeh*	مهریه
Temporary marriage	*sigheh*	صیغه
Secularism	sekolarism/donyāgarayi	سکولاریسم/ دنیاگرایی
Fatwa(s) (religious ruling)	fatvā	فتوا
Qajar (ruling family)	Qājār	قاجار
Reza Shah Pahlavi	Reza Shah Pahlavi	رضا شاه پهلوی
Princess	*Šāhdokht*	شاهدخت
Khedive	*khidēv*	خدیو

GLOSSARY OF ARABIC TERMS

Egyptian Feminist Union	*Al-Ittiḥād Al-Nisāʾī Al-Miṣrī*	الِاتِّحَاد النِّسَائِيّ المِصْرِيّ
Secularism—Derivative of the word *ʿālam* meaning world	*ʿIlmānīyah*	عِلْمَانِيَّة
Women	*An Nisāʾ*	ٱلنِّسَاء
Irrevocable divorce	*ṭalāqun bāʾinun*	طَلَاقٌ بَائِنٌ
House of obedience	*Baytu al-ṭāʿah*	بَيْتُ الطَّاعَةِ
Daughter of the Nile	*Ibnat al-Nīl*	إبْنَةُ النِّيلِ
Religious ruling/legal opinion	*Fatwā*	فَتْوَى
Forbidden sexual behaviour/social disorder/temptation	*Fitnah*	فِتْنَةٌ
A woman's waiting period	*Al-ʿIddah*	الْعِدَّةُ
Waiting period for a widow	*ʿIddat al-Wafāt*	عِدَّةُ الوَفَاةِ
Consensus (of scholars)	Ijmāʿ	إجْمَاعٌ
The leadership of the Muslim community	*Imāmah*	إمَامَةٌ
New Woman Foundation (NWF)/The Society of the New Woman	*Jamʿīyat al-Marʾah al-Jadīdah*	جَمْعِيَّةُ المَرْأَةِ الجَدِيدَةِ

S. Louden-Cooke, *Gender Equality, Matrimony and Secularism in Egypt and Iran: A Comparative Exploration of Early Twentieth-Century Family Law*, Middle East Today, https://doi.org/10.1007/978-3-032-00846-6

The Society for the Literary Advancement of Egyptian Women/The Egyptian Ladies' Literacy Advancement Society	*Jami'at al-Ruqīyy al-Adabī li-l-Sayyidāt al-tala*	جَمْعِيَّةُ الرُّقِيِّ الأَدَبِيِّ لِلسَّيِّدَاتِ المِصْرِيَّاتِ
Sexual jihad	Jihād al-Nikāḥ	جِهَادُ النِّكَاحِ
Dower	*Mahr*	مَهْرٌ
Dowry of equivalent/ Equivalent dower	*Mahr al-Mithl*	مَهْرُ الْمِثْلِ
Amount of dower in case of specific divorce/dowery of temporary marriage	*Mahr al-Mut'ah*	مَهْرُ الْمُتْعَةِ
Egypt	Miṣr	مِصْرُ
Remaining dower payment at time of divorce or death/deferred dowery	*Mu'akkhar*	مُؤَخَّرٌ
Esteemed Muslim scholar	*Mawlā*	مَوْلَى
First half of dower at time of marriage/promote dower	*Muqaddam*	مُقَدَّمٌ
Disobedience/Rebellious wife	*Nāshiz*	نَاشِزٌ
Judge	*Qāḍī*	قَاضِي
Revocable (divorce)	*Rāj'ah*	رَاجِعَةٌ
Chapter (of the Qur'an)	Sūrah	سُورَةٌ
Obedience	*Ṭā'ah*	طَاعَةٌ
Proclamation of divorce	*Ṭalāq*	طَلاقٌ
Innovated divorce	*Ṭalāq al-Bid'ah*	طَلاقُ البِدْعَةِ
Divorce by a third party	*Tāṭlīq*	تَطْلِيقٌ
A body of Muslim scholars	*'ulamā'*	عُلَمَاءُ
Nation/Community	*Ummāh*	أُمَّةٌ
Big Mother	*Umm Kabīrah*	أُمٌّ كَبِيرَةٌ
Non-registered marriage	*'Irfīyy*	عِرْفِيٌّ
Homeland/territory	*Waṭan*	وَطَنٌ
Illicit sexual relations	*Zinā*	زِنَا
Sharia	*Sharī'ah*	الشريعة

Bibliography

Abadan-Unat, N. (1991). The Impact of Legal and Educational Reforms on Turkish Women. In N. R. Keddie & B. Baron (Eds.), *Women in the Middle East: Shifting Boundaries in Sex and Gender* (pp. 177–194). Yale University Press.

Abrahamian, E. (1974). Oriental Despotism: The Case of Qajar Iran. *International Journal of Middle East Studies, 5*(1), 3–31.

Abu-Lughod, L. (1998). Introduction: Feminist Longings and Postcolonial Conditions. In L. Abu-Lughod (Ed.), *Remaking Women: Feminism and Modernity in the Middle East* (pp. 3–31). Princeton University Press.

Abu-Lughod, L. (2001). Review: "Orientalism" and Middle East Feminist Studies. *Feminist Studies, 27*(1), 101–113.

Abu-Odeh, L. (2004). Modernizing Muslim Family Law: The Case of Egypt. *Vanderbilt Journal of Transnational Law, 37*, 1043–1146.

Adib-Moghaddam, A. (2013). What Is Radicalism? Power and Resistance in Iran. In G. Joffé (Ed.), *Islamist Radicalisation in Europe and the Middle East* (pp. 269–299). I.B. Tauris.

Afary, J. (1996). *The Iranian Constitutional Revolution, 1906–1911: Grassroots Democracy, Social Democracy, and the Origins of Feminism.* Columbia University Press.

Afary, J. (1997). The War Against Feminism in the Name of the Almighty: Making Sense of Gender and Muslim Fundamentalism. *New Left Review*, 89–110.

S. Louden-Cooke, *Gender Equality, Matrimony and Secularism in Egypt and Iran: A Comparative Exploration of Early Twentieth-Century Family Law*, Middle East Today, https://doi.org/10.1007/978-3-032-00846-6

Agathangelou, A. M., & Turcotte, H. M. (2010). Postcolonial Theories and Challenges to "First World-ism." In L. J. Shepherd (Ed.), *Gender Matters in Global Politics* (pp. 44–58). Routledge.

Agrama, H. (2010). Secularism, Sovereignty, Interdeterminacy: Is Egypt a Secular or a Religious State? *Comparative Studies in Society and History, 52*(3), 495–523.

Ahmed, L. (1992). *Women and Gender in Islam*. Yale University Press.

Akhavi, S. (1980). *Religion and Politics in Contemporary Iran: Clergy-State Relations in the Pahlavi Period*. State University of New York Press.

Al-Ali, N. (2000). *Secularism, Gender and the State in the Middle East: The Egyptian Women's Movement*. Cambridge University Press.

Ali, A. Y. (2000). *The Holy Qur'an*. Wordsworth Editions Limited.

al-Sultana, T./Vanzan, A., & Neshati, A. (Trans.)/Amanat, A. (Ed.). (n.d./2003). *Crowning Anguish: Memoirs of a Persian Princess from the Harem to Modernity*. Corgi.

Amin, Q. (1899/2000). *The Liberation of Women*. American University of Cairo Press.

Amin, Q. (1900/2000). *The New Woman*. American University of Cairo Press.

Amireh, A. (2000). Framing Nawal El Saadawi: Arab Feminism in a Transnational World. *Signs, 26*(1), 215–249.

Amnesty International. (2014). *Ghoncheh Gavami, in Prison in Iran for Wanting to Watch Volleyball*. Available at: http://www.amnesty.org.uk/ghoncheh-ghavami-prison-iran-volleyball-protest. Retrieved: 1st April 2015.

Amnesty International. (2015). *You Shall Procreate: Attacks on Women's Sexual and Reproductive Rights in Iran*.

Amnesty International. (2018). *Egypt: NGO 'foreign funding' must lead to end of crackdown on human rights community*. Available at: https://www.amnesty.org/en/latest/press-release/2018/12/egypt-ngo-foreign-funding-case-acquittals-must-lead-to-end-of-crackdown-on-human-rights-community/ Retrieved: 31st October 2025.

Anthias, F., & Yuval-Davis, N. (1989). *Woman—Nation—State*. Macmillan.

Anthias, F. (2002). Beyond Feminism and Multiculturalism: Locating Difference and the Politics of Location. *Women's Studies International Forum, 25*(3), 275–286.

Appleby, J., Hunt, L., & Jacob, M. (2011). *Telling the truth about history*. WW Norton & Company.

Asad, T. (2003). *Formations of the Secular: Christianity, Islam, Modernity*. Stanford University Press.

Baderin, M. A. (2001). A Macroscopic Analysis of the Practice of Human Rights Treaties: Conflict or Congruence. *Human Rights Law Review, 1*(2), 265–303.

Badran, M. (1996). *Feminists, Islam, and Nation: Gender and the Making of Modern Egypt*. Princeton University Press.

Badran, M. (2001). Understanding Islam, Islamism, and Islamic Feminism. *Journal of Women's History, 13*(1), 47–52.
Badran, M. (2005). Between Secular and Islamic Feminism/s: Reflections on the Middle East and Beyond. *Journal of Middle East Women's Studies, 1*(1), 6–28.
Badran, M. (2007). *Feminism Beyond East and West: New Gender Talk and Practice in Global Islam*. Global Media Publications.
Badran, M. (2009). *Feminism in Islam: Secular and Religious Convergences*. Oneworld Publications.
Badran, M. (2014). Dis/Playing Power and the Politics of Patriarchy in Revolutionary Egypt: The Creative Activism of Huda Lutfi. *Postcolonial Studies, 17*(1), 47–62.
Bahramitash, R., & Kaziempour, S. (2006). Myths and Realities of the Impact of Islam on Women: Changing Marital Status in Iran. *Critique: Critical Middle Eastern Studies, 15*(2), 111–128.
Bamdad, B. M. (1977). *From Darkness into Light: Women's Emancipation in Iran*. Exposition Press.
Baron, B. (1991). The Making and Breaking of Marital Bonds in Modern Egypt. In N. R. Keddie & B. Baron (Eds.), *Women in the Middle East: Shifting Boundaries in Sex and Gender* (pp. 275–291). Yale University Press.
Baron, B., et al. (1991). Mothers, Morality, and Nationalism in pre-1919 Egypt. In R. Khalidi (Ed.), *The Origins of Arab Nationalism* (pp. 271–288). Columbia University Press.
Baron, B. (1993). The Construction of National Honour in Egypt. *Gender & History, 5*(2), 244–255.
Baron, B. (2005). *Egypt as a Woman: Nationalism, Gender and Politics*. University of California Press.
Başkan, B. (2014). *From Religious Empires to Secular States: State Secularization in Turkey, Iran, and Russia*. Routledge.
Bayat, M. (1991). *Iran's First Revolution: Shi'ism and the Constitutional Revolution of 1905–1909*. Oxford University Press.
Bayat-Philipp, M. (1978). Women and the Revolution in Iran, 1905–1911. In L. Beck & N. R. Keddie (Eds.), *Women in the Muslim World* (pp. 295–308). Harvard University Press.
Baylis, J., & Smith, S. (2005). *The Globalization of World Politics* (3rd ed.). Oxford University Press.
Becker, H. S. (1967). Whose Side Are We On? *Social Problems, 14*(3), pp. 239–247.
Berque, J. (1972). *Egypt*. Faber & Faber Limited.
Bethke Elshtain, J. (1981). *Public Man, Private Woman: Women in Social and Political Thought*. Princeton University Press.

Birla, R. (2010). Postcolonial Studies: Now That's History. In R. C. Morris (Ed.), *Reflections on the History of an Idea: Can the Subaltern Speak?* (pp. 87–99). Columbia University Press.

Bohn, L. (2013). Egypt's marriage crisis: Sons and daughters too broke to be married, waiting for adulthood, *NBC News* Available at: https://www.nbcnews.com/news/world/egypts-marriage-crisis-sons-daughters-too-broke-be-married-waiting-flna2d11711756 Retrieved: 31st October 2025.

Booth, M. (2013). Locating Women's Autobiographical Writing in Colonial Egypt. *Journal of Women's History, 25*(2), 36–60.

Botman, S. (1991). *Egypt from Independence to Revolution, 1919–1952.* Syracuse University Press.

Bourke, B. (2014). Positionality: Reflecting on the Research Process. *The Qualitative Report, 19*(33), 1–9.

Briggs, J., & Sharp, J. (2004). Indigenous Knowledges and Development: A Postcolonial Caution. *Third World Quarterly, 25*(4), 661–676.

Browne, E. G. (1910). *The Persian Revolution of 1905–1909.* University Press.

Chakrabarty, D. (2000). *Provincializing Europe: Postcolonial Thought and Historical Difference.* Princeton University Press.

Chakraborty, M. N. (2007). Wa(i)ving It All Away: Producing Subject and Knowledge in Feminisms of Colours. In S. Gillis, G. Howie, & R. Munford (Eds.), *Third Wave Feminism: A Critical Exploration* (pp. 101–113). Palgrave Macmillan.

Cohn, C. (2013). Women and Wars: Toward a Conceptual Framework. In C. Cohn (Ed.), *Women & Wars* (pp. 1–35). Polity Press.

Colliver-Rice, C. (1923). *Persian Women and Their Ways.* Seeley, Service & Co. Limited.

Connell, R. W. (1987). *Gender & Power.* Polity Press.

Cooke, M. (2001). *Women Claim Islam.* Routledge.

Cooke, S. (2020). Power, Secularism and Divorce: Women's Rights in Egypt and Iran. *National Identities, 22*(5), 479–497 (IF 0.59). https://doi.org/10.1080/14608944.2019.1634034

Cooke, S. (2021). Secular Identities: An Exploration of Secular Models in Islam. In S. Raudino & U. Ashraf Barton (Eds.), *Abraham and the Secular* (pp. 195–220). Palgrave Macmillan.

Cottam, R. W. (1979). *Nationalism in Iran: Updated Through 1978.* University of Pittsburgh Press.

Coulson, N., & Hinchcliffe, D. (1978). Women and Law Reform in Contemporary Iran. In L. Beck & N. R. Keddie (Eds.), *Women in the Muslim World* (pp. 37–51). Harvard University Press.

Cronin, S. (1997). *The Army and the Creation of the Pahlavi State in Iran, 1910–1926.* I.B. Tauris.

D'Costa, B. (2006). Marginalized Identity: New Frontiers of Research for IR? In B. A. Ackerly, M. Stern, & J. True (Eds.), *Feminist Methodologies for International Relations* (pp. 129–152). Cambridge University Press.

De Groot, J. (1996). Gender, Discourse and Ideology in Iranian Studies: Towards a New Scholarship. In D. Kandiyoti (Ed.), *Gendering the Middle East: Emerging Perspectives* (pp. 29–50). I.B. Tauris.

Demerath, J. (2007). Secularization and Sacralization Deconstructed and Reconstructed. In J. A. Beckford & N. J. Demerath (Eds.), *The SAGE Handbook of Religion*. Sage.

Dunne, B. (1998). Power and Sexuality in the Middle East. *Middle East Report* (206), 8–11 + 37.

Eaton, G. (1994). *Islam and the Destiny of Man*. The Islamic Texts Society.

ecwronline.org. (2012). *Egypt Fears for Girls, Marriage Laws in New Constitution*. Available at: http://ecwronline.org/?p=829. Retrieved: 29th June 2015.

Efrati, N. (2005). Negotiating Rights in Iraq: Women and Personal Status Law. *Middle East Journal, 59*(4), 577–595.

Eickelman, D. F., & Salvatore, A. (2002). The Public Sphere and Muslim Identities. *European Journal of Sociology, 43*(1), 92–115.

Eisenstein, Z. R. (1979). Developing a Theory of Capitalist Patriarchy and Socialist Feminism. In Z. R. Eisenstein (Ed.), *Capitalist Patriarchy and the Case for Socialist Feminism* (pp. 5–49). Monthly Review Press.

Eisenstein, Z. R. (1981). *The Radical Future of Liberal Feminism*. Longman Inc.

El Guindi, F. (2003). Veiling Resistance. In R. Lewis & S. Mills (Eds.), *Feminist Postcolonial Theory: A Reader* (pp. 586–609). Edinburgh University Press.

Eley, G. (1992). Nations, Publics, and Political Cultures: Placing Habermas in the Nineteenth Century. In C. Calhoun (Ed.), *Habermas and the Public Sphere*. MIT Press.

Engineer, A. (2008). *Rights of Women in Islam* (3rd ed.). Stirling Publishers Private Limited.

English Text of the Proclamation of 1914. (1919). *British Foreign and State Papers* (109), 436.

Entelis, J. (1996). International Human Rights: Islam's Friend or Foe? Algeria as an Example of the Compatibility of International Human Rights regarding Women's Equality and Islamic Law. *Fordham International Law Journal, 20*, 1251–1305.

Eshkevari, H. Y. (2013). Rethinking Men's Authority over Women: *Qiwāma, Wilāya* and their Underlying Assumptions. In Z. Mir-Hosseini et al. (Eds.), *Gender and Equality in Muslim Family Law: Justice and Ethics in Islamic Legal Tradition* (pp. 191–212). I.B. Tauris.

Fanon, F. (1963). *The Wretched of the Earth*. Penguin Books.

Fanon, F. (1967). *Toward the African Revolution*. Grove Press Inc.

Farid, M./Goldschmidt, A. (Trans.). (1992). *The Memoirs and Diaries of Muhammad Farid, an Egyptian Nationalist Leader (1868–1919)*. Mellen University Research Press.

Farman Farmaian, S. (1993). *Daughter of Persia: A Woman's Journey from Her Father's Harem Through the Islamic Revolution*. Corgi.

Fay, M. A. (2003). From Warrior-Grandees to Domesticated Bourgeoisie: The Transformation of the Elite Egyptian Household into a Western-Style Nuclear Family. In B. Doumani (Ed.), *Family History in the Middle East: Household, Property, and Gender* (pp. 77–100). State University of New York Press.

Felski, R. (1995). *The Gender of Modernity*. Harvard University Press.

Ferdows, A. K. (1985). The Status and Rights of Women in Ithna 'Ashari Shi'i Islam. In A. Fathi (Ed.), *Women and the Family in Iran*. E.J. Brill.

Ferrara, A. (2009). The Separation of Religion and Politics in a Post-secular Society. *Philosophy and Social Criticism, 35*(1–2), 77–91.

FIS. (n.d.). *Iran's 1906 Constitution*. Available at: http://fisiran.org/en/resources/legaldoc/iranconstitution. Retrieved: 1st April 2015.

FIS. *2007 Family Protection Bill*. Available at: http://fisiran.org/en/women/laws/07fb. Retrieved: 29th June 2015.

Fischer, M. M. J. (1978). On Changing the Concept and Position of Persian Women. In L. Beck & N. R. Keddie (Eds.), *Women in the Muslim World* (pp. 189–215). Harvard University Press.

Fluehr-Lobban, C. (1980). The Political Mobilization of Women in the Arab World. In J. I. Smith (Ed.), *Women in Contemporary Muslim Societies* (pp. 235–252). Bucknell University Press.

FO 141/511/5. (1921). *Political Views and Activities of Egyptian Women*. TNA.

FO 141/511/6. (1924). *Political Views and Activities of Certain Egyptian Women, Particularly Madame Esther Fahmy Wissa of Women Wafd Committee and Madame Huda Hanem Sharawi*. TNA.

FO 141/792/4. (1927). *Egyptian Divorce Laws*. TNA.

FO 416/112. (1932). *Persia Annual Reports 1922–1926*. TNA.

Fokas, E. (2010). Secularism and Secularity: Contemporary International Perspectives. *Culture and Religion: An Interdisciplinary Journal, 11*(2), 163–169.

Foran, J. (1989). The Concept of Dependent Development as a Key to the Political Economy of Qajar Iran (1800–1925). *Iranian Studies, 22*(2/3), 5–56.

Foran, J. (1998). Dangerous Populations? Concepts for the Comparative Study of Social Movements in Qajar Iran. *Critique: Critical Middle Eastern Studies, 7*(13), 3–27.

Foucault, M. (1980). *Power/Knowledge: Selected Interviews 1972–77* (C. Gordon, Ed.). Harvester.

Foucault, M. (1982). The Subject and Power. *Critical Inquiry, 8*(4), 777–795.

Friedl, E. (1991). The Dynamics of Women's Spheres of Action in Rural Iran. In N. R. Keddie & B. Baron (Eds.), *Women in the Middle East: Shifting Boundaries in Sex and Gender* (pp. 195–214). Yale University Press.

Freire, P. (2000). *Pedagogy of the Oppressed*. Continuum.

Gellner, D. N. (2001). Studying Secularism, Practising Secularism: Anthropological Imperatives. *Social Anthropology, 9*(3), 337–340.

Ghani, C. (1998). *Iran and the Rise of Reza Shah: From Qajar Collapse to Pahlavi Power*. I.B. Tauris.

Ghobadi, P., Binley, A., & Williams, N. (2022). *Evin prison fire: Several dead after fire at Iran's notorious detention centre*, BBC. Available at: https://www.bbc.co.uk/news/world-asia-63271817 Retrieved 30th October 2025

Gillis, S., Howie, G., & Munford, R. (2007). Introduction. In S. Gillis, G. Howie, & R. Munford (Eds.), *Third Wave Feminism: A Critical Exploration* (pp. xxi–xxxiv). Palgrave Macmillan.

Göl, A. (2009). The Identity of Turkey: Muslim and Secular. *Third World Quarterly, 30*(4), 795–811.

Goldschmidt, A. (2000). *Biographical Dictionary of Modern Egypt*. Lynne Rienner.

Goldstein, E. (2002). *The First World War Peace Settlements 1919–1925*. Pearson Education Limited.

Goodrich T. J. (1991). Women, power, and family therapy: What's wrong with this picture? *Journal of Feminist Family Therapy*, 3, 5–37.

Grant, A. (2018). Shock and offence online: The role of emotion in participant absent research. In *Emotion and the Researcher: Sites, Subjectivities, and Relationships*, pp. 143–158. Emerald Publishing Limited.

Grant, R., & Newland, K. (Eds.). (1991). *Gender and International Relations*. Indiana University Press.

Habermas, J. (1962/1989). *The Structural Transformation of the Public Sphere: An Inquiry into a Category of Bourgeois Society*. MIT Press.

Hafez, S. (2011). *An Islam of Her Own*. New York University Press.

Hallaq, W. B. (2005). *The Origins and Evolution of Islamic Law*. Cambridge University Press.

Halliday, F. (2003). *Islam and the Myth of Confrontation*. I.B. Tauris.

Harik, R. M., & Marston, E. (1996). *Women in the Middle East: Tradition and Change*. Franklin Watts.

Hashemi, N. (2010). The Multiple Histories of Secularism: Muslim Societies in Comparison. *Philosophy and Social Criticism, 36*(3–4), 325–338.

Hassan, H. (2000). *In the House of Muhammad Ali: A Family Album, 1805–1952*. The American University in Cairo Press.

Hasso, F. S. (2011). *Consuming Desires: Family Crisis and the State in the Middle East*. Stanford University Press.

Hatem, M. F. (1989). Through Each Other's Eyes: Egyptian, Levantine-Egyptian, and European Women's Images of Themselves and of Each Other (1862–1920). *Women's Studies International Forum, 12*(2), 183–198.

Hatem, M. F. (1994). Egyptian Discourses on Gender and Political Liberalization: Do Secularist and Islamist Views Really Differ? *Middle East Journal, 48*(4), 661–676.

Hegde, R. S. (1998). A View from Elsewhere: Locating Difference and the Politics of Representation from a Transnational Feminist Perspective. *Communication Theory, 8*(3), 271–297.

Hermann, D. (2013). Akhund Khurasani and the Iranian Constitutional Movement. *Middle Eastern Studies, 49*(3), 430–453.

Hibbard, S. W. (2010). *Religious Politics and Secular States: Egypt, India, and the United States.* The Johns Hopkins University Press.

Higgins, P. J. (1985). Women in the Islamic Republic of Iran: Legal, Social, and Ideological Changes. *Signs, 10*(3), 477–494.

Holt, M. (2010). Agents of Defiance and Despair: The Impact of Islamic Resistance on Palestinian Women in the West Bank and Gaza Strip. *Totalitarian Movements and Political Religions, 11*(3–4), 397–415.

hooks, b. (1984). *Feminist Theory: From Margin to Centre* (2nd ed.). South End Press Classics.

Htun, M., & Weldon, S. L. (2010). When Do Governments Promote Women's Rights? A Framework for the Comparative Analysis of Sex Equality. *Perspectives on Politics, 8*(1), 207–216.

Hunter, A. (2007). *Power and Passion in Egypt: A Life of Sir Eldon Gorst, 1861–1911.* I.B. Tauris.

Ismail, S. (1998). Confronting the Other: Identity, Culture, Politics, and Conservative Islamism in Egypt. *International Journal of Middle East Studies, 30*(2), 199–225.

Jackson, S. A. (2024). *The Islamic Secular.* Oxford University Press.

Jacobs, J. M. (2003). Earth Honoring: Western Desires and Indigenous Knowledges. In R. Lewis & S. Mills (Eds.), *Feminist Postcolonial Theory: A Reader* (pp. 667–691). Edinburgh University Press.

Jayawardena, K. (1986). *Feminism and Nationalism in the Third World.* Zed Books.

Joseph, S. (1996). Gender and Citizenship in Middle Eastern States. *Middle East Report, 198*, 4–10.

Juergensmeyer, M. (1993). *The New Cold War? Religious Nationalism Confronts the Secular State.* University of California Press.

Kamali Dehgan, S. (2015). British-Iranian woman jailed over volleyball game sees charges dropped, *The Guardian* Available at: https://www.theguardian.com/world/2015/apr/02/british-iranian-goncheh-ghavami-jailed-volleyball-game-charges-dropped-iran Retrieved: 31st October 2025.

Kandiyoti, D. (1991). Islam and Patriarchy: A Comparative Perspective. In N. R. Keddie & B. Baron (Eds.), *Women in the Middle East: Shifting Boundaries in Sex and Gender* (pp. 23–42). Yale University Press.

Kandiyoti, D. (Ed.). (1996). *Gendering the Middle East: Emerging Perspectives*. I.B. Tauris.

Kapur, R. (2002). The Tragedy of Victimization Rhetoric: Ressurecting the "Native" Subject in International/Post-Colonial Feminist Legal Politics. *Harvard Human Rights Journal, 15*, 1–37.

Karmi, G. (2005). Women, Islam and Patriarchalism. In H. Moghissi (Ed.), *Women and Islam: Image and Reality* (pp. 165–178). Routledge.

Kaufman, M. (1994). Men, Feminism, and Men's Contradictory Experiences of Power. In H. Brod & M. Kaufman (Eds.), *Theorizing Masculinities*. Sage.

Keddie, N. R. (1969). Iranian Politics 1900–1905: Background to Revolution. *Middle Eastern Studies, 5*(1), 3–31.

Keddie, N. R. (1999). *Qajar Iran and the Rise of Reza Khan 1796–1925*. Mazda Publishers.

Keddie, N. R. (2001). *Women in Iran Since 1979*. Women Living Under Muslim Laws, Dossier 23.

Keddie, N. R. (2003). Secularism & Its Discontents. *Daedalus, 132*(3), 14–30.

Kedourie, E. (1993). *Nationalism*. Wiley.

Kezar, A. (2002). Reconstructing Static Images of Leadership: An Application of Positionality Theory. *Journal of Leadership Studies, 8*(3), 94–109.

Kholoussy, H. (2003). Stolen Husbands, Foreign Wives: Mixed Marriage, Identity Formation and Gender in Colonial Egypt, 1909–1923. *Hawwa, 1*(2), 206–240.

Kholoussy, H. (2010). *For Better, for Worse: The Marriage Crisis That Made Modern Egypt*. Stanford University Press.

Knell, Y. (2010, January 19). *The Perils of Young Egyptian's Secret Marriages*. BBC. Available at: http://news.bbc.co.uk/1/hi/world/middle_east/8466188.stm. Retrieved: 8th August 2015.

Kosmin, B. A. (2007). Introduction: Contemporary Secularity and Secularism. In B. A. Kosmin & A. Keysar (Eds.), *Secularism and Secularity: Contemporary International Perspectives* (pp. 1–16). ISSSC.

Kurzman, C. (Ed.). (2002). *Modernist Islam, 1840–1940: A Source Book*. Oxford University Press.

Lambert, I., & Ramadan, N. (2015, July 2). *Who's the Daddy? Ezz, Zeina and Egypt's Urfi Marriages*. al-Araby. Available at: http://www.alaraby.co.uk/english/blog/2015/7/2/whos-the-daddy-ezz-zeina-and-egypts-urfi-marriages. Retrieved: 8th August 2015.

Landes, J. B. (2003). Further Thoughts on the Public/Private Distinction. *Journal of Women's History, 15*(2), 28–39.

Lazreg, M. (1988). Feminism and Difference: The Perils of Writing as a Woman in Algeria. *Feminist Studies, 14*(1), 81–107.

Lazreg, M. (1994). Women's Experience and Feminist Epistemology: A Critical Neo-rationalist Approach. In K. Lennon & M. Whitford (Eds.), *Knowing Difference: Feminist Perspectives in Epistemology* (pp. 45–62). Routledge.

Lewis, R., & Mills, S. (2003). Introduction. In R. Lewis & S. Mills (Eds.), *Feminist Postcolonial Theory: A Reader* (pp. 1–22). Edinburgh University Press.

Loft, P. (2023). *One-year anniversary of the Mahsa Amini protests in Iran*, House of Commons Library. Available at: https://commonslibrary.parliament.uk/one-year-anniversary-of-the-mahsa-amini-protests-in-iran/ Retrieved: 30th October 2025

Lombardi, C. B. (1998). Islamic Law as a Source of Constitutional Law in Egypt: The Constitutionalization of the Sharia in a Modern Arab State. *Columbia Journal of Transnational Law, 37*, 81–123.

Louden-Cooke, S. (2024). Power, Politics & Resistance: Secularism and Women's Marital Rights in Egypt and Iran. *British Journal of Middle Eastern Studies, 55*(5), 1011–1030 (IF 0.972). https://doi.org/10.1080/13530194.2023.2185591

Mack-Canty, C. (2004). Third-Wave Feminism and the Need to Reweave the Nature/Culture Identity. *NWSA Journal, 16*(3), 154–179.

Maerz, M. (2011). Lara Logan breaks her silence on '60 Minutes': 'They raped me with their hands', *Los Angeles Times* Available at: https://www.latimes.com/archives/blogs/show-tracker/story/2011-05-02/lara-logan-breaks-her-silence-on-60-minutes-they-raped-me-with-their-hands Retrieved: 31st October 2025.

Marashi, A. (2008). *Nationalizing Iran: Culture, Power, and the State, 1870–1940*. University of Washington Press.

McEwan, C. (2001). Postcolonialism, Feminism and Development: Intersections and Dilemmas. *Progress in Development Studies, 1*(2), 91–111.

McNay, L. (1992). *Foucault and Feminism: Power, Gender and the Self*. Polity Press.

Megahead, N., & Lack, S. (2013). Women's Rights and Gender Educational Inequality in Egypt and Tunisia. In *Education, Dominance, and Identity* (pp. 201–222). SensePublishers.

Mernissi, F. (1991). *The Veil and the Male Elite: A Feminist Interpretation of Women's Rights in Islam*. Basic Books.

Milani, F. (1992). *Veils and Words: The Emerging Voices of Iranian Women Writers*. Syracuse University Press.

Mills, S. (2003). Gender and Colonial Space. In R. Lewis & S. Mills (Eds.), *Feminist Postcolonial Theory: A Reader* (pp. 692–719). Edinburgh University Press.

Mills, S. (2005). *Gender and Colonial Space*. Manchester University Press.

Mir-Hosseini, Z. (2006). Muslim Women's Quest for Equality: Between Islamic Law and Feminism. *Critical Inquiry, 32*(4), 629–645.

Mir-Hosseini, Z. (2009). Towards Gender Equality: Muslim Family Laws and the Shari'ah. *WANTED*, 23–63.

Mir-Hosseini, Z. (2012). Politics of Divorce Laws in Iran: Ideology Versus Practice. In R. Mehdi, W. Menski, & J. S. Nielsen (Eds.), *Interpreting Divorce Laws in Islam* (pp. 65–83). DJOF Publishing.

Mir-Hosseini, Z., et al. (2013), Muslim Family Law and the Question of Equality. In Z. Mir-Hosseini et al. (Eds.), *Gender and Equality in Muslim Family Law: Justice and Ethics in the Islamic Legal Tradition* (pp. 1–6). I.B. Tauris.

Moaddel, M. (1998). Religion and Women: Islamic Modernism Versus Fundamentalism. *Journal for the Scientific Study of Religion, 37*(1), 108–130.

Moaddel, M., & Azardarmaki, T. (2002). The Worldviews of Islamic Publics: The Cases of Egypt, Iran, and Jordan. *Comparative Sociology, 1*(3), 299–319.

Moghadam, V. M. (2004). Patriarchy in Transition: Women and the Changing Family in the Middle East. *Journal of Comparative Family Studies, 35*(2), 137–162.

Moghadam, V. M. (2013). *Modernizing Women: Gender and Social Change in the Middle East* (3rd ed.). Lynne Rienner Publishers Inc.

Moghissi, H. (1999). *Feminism and Islamic Fundamentalism: The Limits of Post Modern Analysis*. Zed Books.

Moghissi, H. (2005). *Women and Islam: Image and Reality*. Routledge.

Mohanty, C. T. (1988). Under Western eyes: Feminist scholarship and colonial discourses. *Feminist review, 30*(1), 61–88.

Mohanty, C. T. (2003a). "Under Western Eyes" Revisited: Feminist Solidarity Through Anticapitalist Struggles. *Signs, 2*, 499–535.

Mohanty, C. T. (2003b). Under Western Eyes: Feminist Scholarship and Colonial Discourses. In R. Lewis & S. Mills (Eds.), *Feminist Postcolonial Theory: A Reader* (pp. 49–74). Edinburgh University Press.

Mojab, S. (2001). Theorizing the Politics of 'Islamic Feminism.' *Feminist Review, 69*(1), 124–146.

Moslem Marriage and Divorce: Text of the New Law. (1929, March). *The Egyptian Gazette*, 4.

Najjar, F. M. (1996). The Debate on Islam and Secularism in Egypt. *Arab Studies Quarterly, 1*(2), 1–22.

Najmabadi, A. (1991). Hazards of Modernity and Morality: Women, State and Ideology in Contemporary Iran. In *Women, Islam and the State* (pp. 48–76). Springer.

Najmabadi, A. (2000). (Un)Veiling Feminism. *Social Text, 18*(3), 29–45.

Naqvi, A. R. (1967). The Family Protection Act of Iran. *Islamic Studies, 6*(3), 241–265.

Naqvi, A. R. (1968a). The Family Laws of Iran (II). *Islamic Studies, 7*(2), 129–163.

Naqvi, A. R. (1968b). The Family Laws of Iran (III). *Islamic Studies, 7*(3), 265–303.

Naqvi, A. R. (1968c). The Family Laws of Iran (IV). *Islamic Studies, 7*(4), 339–378.

Nazir, S. (2005). Challenging Inequality: Obstacles and Opportunities Towards Women's Rights in the Middle East and North Africa. *JIJIS, 5*, 31–42.

Nelson, C. (1996). *Doria Shafik, Egyptian Feminist: A Woman Apart*. The American University in Cairo Press.

NWRO. (n.d.). *Legal Guide for Developing a More Just Integrated Family Law*. Available at: www.powregypt.org/upload/Family_law_Eng.pdf. Retrieved: 1st April 2015.

Olsen, F. E. E. (1993). International Law: Feminist Critiques of the Public/ Private Distinction. *Studies in Transnational Legal Policy, 25*, 157–169.

Paidar, P. (1996). Feminism and Islam in Iran. In D. Kandiyoti (Ed.), *Gendering the Middle East*. I.B. Tauris.

Parvis-Brookshaw, D. (2013). Women in Praise of Women: Female Poets and Female Patrons in Qajar Iran. *Iranian Studies, 46*(1), 17–48.

Pateman, C. (1988). *The Sexual Contract*. Polity Press.

Peaslee, A. J. (1950a). Constitution of Egypt. In *Constitutions of Nations: Afghanistan to Finland* (pp. 721–735). Rumford Press.

Peaslee, A. J. (1950b). Iranian Constitutional Law. In *Constitutions of Nations: France to Poland* (pp. 206–213). Rumford Press.

Peaslee, A. J. (1950c). The Iranian Constitution. In *Constitutions of Nations: France to Poland* (pp. 200–205). Rumford Press.

Pickthall, M. (1973/2012). *The Meaning of the Glorious Qur'an*. I.D.C.I.

Pillow, W. (2003). Confession, Catharsis, or Cure? Rethinking the Uses of Reflexivity as Methodological Power in Qualitative Research. *International Journal of Qualitative Studies in Education, 16*(2), 175–196.

Qutb, S., Salahi, A., & Shamis, A. (Eds.). (2001). *In the Shade of the Qur'an* (Vol. 3). The Islamic Foundation.

Rabinow, P. (2008). Midst Anthropology's Problems. *Cultural Anthropology, 17*(2), 135–149.

Rahnema, A., & Nomani, F. (1990). *The Secular Miracle: Religion, Politics & Economic Policy in Iran*. Zed Books.

Rajan, R. S. (1993). *Real & Imagined Women*. Routledge.

Ramazanoğlu, C. (2002). *Feminist Methodology: Challenges and Choices*. Sage.

Raven-Roberts, A. (2013). Women and the Political Economy of War. In C. Cohn (Ed.), *Women & Wars* (pp. 36–53). Polity Press.

Regan, C. (1985). Ahmad Kasravi's Views on the Role of Women in Iranian Society as Expressed in Our Sister's and Daughters. In A. Fathi (Ed.), *Women and the Family in Iran* (pp. 60–76). E.J. Brill.

Reilly, N. (2011). Rethinking the Interplay of Feminism and Secularism in a Neo-Secular Age. *Feminist Review, 97*(1), 5–31.

R.I.I.A. (1952). *Great Britain and Egypt: 1914–1951: Information Papers No. 19.* Oxford University Press.

Ryan, M. P. (1992). Gender and Public Access: Women's Politics in Nineteenth Century America. In C. Calhoun (Ed.), *Habermas and the Public Sphere.* MIT Press.

Sa'ar, A. (2005). Postcolonial Feminism, the Politics of Identification, and the Liberal Bargain. *Gender and Society, 19*(5), 680–700.

Sabit, A. M. (1989). *A King Betrayed: The Ill-Fated Reign of Farouk of Egypt.* Quartet Books Limited.

Sadiqi, F., & Ennaji, M. (2011). *Women in the Middle East and North Africa: Agents of Change.* Routledge.

Said, E. (1978/2003). *Orientalism.* Penguin Books.

Saliba, T., Allen, C., & Howard, J. A. (Eds.). (2002). *Gender, Politics, and Islam.* The University of Chicago Press.

Sanasarian, E. (1982). *The Women's Rights Movement in Iran: Mutiny, Appeasement, and Repression from 1900 to Khomeini.* Praeger.

Sanasarian, E. (1985). Characteristics of Women's Movement in Iran. In A. Fathi (Ed.), *Women and the Family in Iran* (pp. 86–106). E.J. Brill.

Sanders, P. (1991). Gendering the Ungendered Body: Hermaphrodites in Medieval Islamic Law. In N. R. Keddie & B. Baron (Eds.), *Women in the Middle East: Shifting Boundaries in Sex and Gender* (pp. 74–95). Yale University Press.

Schutte, O. (1998). Cultural Alterity: Cross-Cultural Communication and Feminist Theory in North-South Contexts. *Hypatia, 13*(2), 53–72.

Scott, J. C. (1985). *Weapons of the weak: Everyday forms of peasant resistance.* Yale University Press.

Shaarawi, H./Badran, M. (Ed.). *Harem Years: The Memoirs of an Egyptian Feminist (1879–1924).* Feminist Press at the City University of New York.

Shaham, R. (1999). State, Feminists and Islamists: The Debate over Stipulations in the Marriage Contracts in Egypt. *Bulletin of the School of Oriental and African Studies, 62*(3), 462–483.

Shahidian, H. (2002). *Women in Iran: Emerging Voices in the Women's Movement.* Greenwood Publishing.

Shail, A. (2007). "You're Not One of Those Boring Masculinists, Are You?' The Question of Male-Embodied Feminism. In S. Gillis, G. Howie, & R. Munford (Eds.), *Third Wave Feminism: A Critical Exploration* (pp. 86–100). Palgrave Macmillan.

Shakry, O. (1998). Schooled Mothers and Structured Play: Child Rearing in Turn-of-the-Century Egypt. In L. Abu-Lughod (Ed.), *Remaking Women: Feminism and Modernity in the Middle East* (pp. 126–170). Princeton University Press.

Sharawi Lanfranchi, S. (2012). *Casting off the Veil: The Life of Huda Shaarawi, Egypt's First Feminist*. I.B. Tauris.

Sonbol, A. (Ed./Trans.). (1998). *The Last Khedive of Egypt: Memoirs of Abbas Hilmi II*. Ithica Press.

Spivak, G. C. (2010). Can the Subaltern Speak? In R. C. Morris (Ed.), *Reflections on the History of an Idea: Can the Subaltern Speak?* (pp. 21–78). Columbia University Press.

Stanley, L., & Wise, S. (1993). *Breaking Out Again* (2nd ed.). Routledge and Kegan Paul Ltd.

Stimpson, C. R. (1988). Nancy Reagan Wears a Hat: Feminism and Its Cultural Consensus. *Critical Inquiry, 14*(2), 223–243.

Strong, S. (1997). Law and Religion in Israel and Iran: How the Integration of Secular and Spiritual Laws Affects Human Rights and the Potential for Violence. *Michigan Journal of International Law, 19*, 109–217.

Sullivan, Z. T. (1998). Eluding the Feminist, Overthrowing the Modern? Transformations in Twentieth-Century Iran. In L. Abu-Lughod (Ed.), *Remaking Women: Feminism and Modernity in the Middle East* (pp. 215–242). Princeton University Press.

Susen, S. (2011). Critical Notes on Habermas's Theory of the Public Sphere. *Sociological Analysis, 5*(1), 37–62.

Tabari, A. (1983). The Role of the Clergy in Modern Iranian Politics. In N. R. Keddie (Ed.), *Religion and Politics in Iran: Shi'ism from Quietism to Revolution* (pp. 47–72). Yale University Press.

Taleghany, M. A. R. (1995). *The Civil Code of Iran*. Fred B. Rothman.

Talhami, G. H. (1996). *The Mobilization of Muslim Women in Egypt*. University Press of Florida.

Tavakoli-Targhi, M. (1990). Refashioning Iran: Language and Culture During the Constitutional Revolution. *Iranian Studies, 23*(1/4), 77–101.

Taylor, C. (2007). *A Secular Age*. The Belknap Press of Harvard University Press.

The Guardian. (2014). Iranian-British woman jailed for attending volleyball match bailed (November 23rd 2014), *The Guardian*. Available at: http://www.theguardian.com/world/2014/nov/23/iranian-british-woman-jailed-attending-iran-volleyball-match-bailed Retrieved: April 1st 2015

The Persian Constitution. (n.d.). *British Foreign and State Papers 1907–1908* (pp. 527–542).

Tickner, A. (2006). Feminism Meets International Relations: Some Methodological Issues. In B. A. Ackerly, M. Stern, & J. True (Eds.), *Feminist*

Methodologies for International Relations (pp. 19–41). Cambridge University Press.

Tickner, J. A., & Sjoberg, L. (2013). Feminism. In T. Dunne, M. Kurki, & S. Smith (Eds.), *International Relations Theories: Discipline and Diversity* (pp. 205–222). Oxford University Press.

Tignor, R. L. (1976). The Egyptian Revolution of 1919: New Directions in the Egyptian Economy. *Middle Eastern Studies, 12*(3), 41–67.

Tohidi, N. (2003). *Islamic Feminism: "Perils and Promises."* Middle Eastern Women on the Move, 135–146.

Torstrick, R. L. (2003). Women and Power in the Middle East, and: Secularism, Gender and the State in the Middle East: The Egyptian Women's Movement, and: Unveiling Traditions: Postcolonial Islam in a Polycentric World (Review). *NWSA Journal, 15*(1), 160–164.

Tripp, C. (1996). Islam and the Secular Logic of the State in the Middle East. In A. S. Sidahmed & A. Ehteshami (Eds.), *Islamic Fundamentialism* (pp. 51–69). Westview Press.

Tripp, C. (2013). *The Power and the People: Paths of Resistance in the Middle East.* Cambridge University Press.

UN Women Justice Report: Get the Data. (2011). *The Guardian.* Available at: http://www.theguardian.com/global-development/poverty-matters/2011/jul/06/un-women-legal-rights-data. Retrieved: 29th June 2015.

UN. (2024). HRC Press Conference–Fact Finding Mission Report on Iran–8 March 2024 Available at: https://www.unognewsroom.org/story/en/2100/hrc-press-conference-fact-finding-mission-report-on-iran-18-march-2024#:~:text=%E2%80%9DWhat%20we%20found%20was%20that,intersecting%20with%20ethnicity%20and%20religion. Retrieved: 31st October 2025

Urry, A. (2011). The Struggle Towards a Feminist Practice in Family Therapy: Premises. In R. Jozef Perelberg & A. C. Miller (Eds.), *Gender and Power in Families* (3rd ed., pp. 104–134). Karnac Books Ltd.

Vatandoust, G. (1985). The Status of Iranian Women During the Pahlavi Regime. In A. Fathi (Ed.), *Women and the Family in Iran* (pp. 107–130). E.J. Brill.

Walby, S. (1989). Theorising Patriarchy. *Sociology, 23*(2), 213–234.

Walters, M. (2011). A Feminist Perspective in Family Therapy. In R. Jozef Perelberg & A. C. Miller (Eds.), *Gender and Power in Families* (3rd ed., pp. 13–33). Karnac Books Ltd.

Weber, M. (1947). *The Theory of Social and Economic Organisation.* New York: Free Press.

Weingartner, L. A. (2004). Family Law & Reform in Morocco—The Mudawana: Modernsit Islam and Women's Rights in the Code of Personal Status. *University of Detroit Mercy Law Review* (82), 687–713.

Werbner, P., & Yuval-Davis, N. (1999). Women and the New Discourse of Citizenship. In P. Werbner & N. Yuval-Davis (Eds.), *Women, Citizenship and Difference*. Zed Books.

Wollstonecraft, M. (1792/2004). *A Vindication of the Rights of Woman*. Penguin Books.

Wright, H. F. (1919a). English Translation of the Organic Law of 1913. In *Constitutions of the States at War* (pp. 175–190). US Government Printing Office.

Wright, H. F. (1919b). *The Constitutions of the States at War, 1914–1918*. US Government Printing Office.

Yeğenoğlu, M. (1998). *Colonial Fantasies: Towards a Feminist Reading of Orientalism*. Cambridge University Press.

Yoder, J. D., & Kahn, A. S. (1992). Toward a Feminist Understanding of Women and Power. *Psychology of Women Quarterly, 16*(4), 381–388.

Yuval-Davis, N. (2013). *Politics and Culture Series, Volume 49: Gender and Nation*. Sage.

Index

S. Louden-Cooke, *Gender Equality, Matrimony and Secularism in Egypt and Iran: A Comparative Exploration of Early Twentieth-Century Family Law*, Middle East Today, https://doi.org/10.1007/978-3-032-00846-6

FSC
www.fsc.org
MIX
Papier | Fördert
gute Waldnutzung
FSC® C083411

Kolibri 360 GmbH
Ferdinand-Jühlke-Straße 7
99095 Erfurt, Deutschland
produktsicherheit@kolibri360.de